Misak Terzibasiyan

UArchitects

20 YEARS

JOURNEY OF A STUDIO

Built Projects

Volume 1

INTRODUCTION

Some years ago, I had the pleasure of speaking with Harm Tilman, chief editor of de Architect, a prominent Dutch magazine on architecture. During this fascinating conversation, I was triggered by his question why the -ism in architecture seems to have disappeared?
It was a rhetorical question, of course, because he already had his view on the matter. If I look back at the time while I was studying at the University of Eindhoven (1985-1991), an international mainstream of architecture magazines dominated the landscape, without the enormous influence of internet and social media through their seductive images.

As part of my master's degree, I studied at the sustainable architecture department. It wasn't fashionable at all in those days to study architecture that had been influenced or motivated by sustainability, but I was fascinated nonetheless by the holistic and sustainable approach of my professor, Peter Schmid. Later in life, this formed a basis for the new work, which you will be able to read in Volume 2 that is due for release in 2026.

You were able to comprehend architecture in the eighties and nineties by reading literature and the latest architectural magazines that focused on interesting new projects.

The main difference with today is that architectural critics and experts back then would filter the architectural quality of the projects. Reviews were critical and fundamentally oriented on the content, making it easier to understand the meaning of architecture. For me, these were a great source of knowledge to learn what was happening in the Netherlands and internationally. It was during my studies that I first encountered architectural movements such as post-modernism and deconstructivism.

I was fascinated by Aldo Rossi, Frank Gehry, James Stirling, Rem Koolhaas and upcoming Swiss architects like Herzog & de Meuron. The early works of these architects were truly remarkable, offering an entirely new and conceptual view. It took some time to understand the thinking behind their work by studying, reading and visiting their projects. But all that time and effort during this educational period was an incredible experience. The impact and significance that architecture can have is profound.

These periods have shaped me as an architect, especially the first 2.5 years after graduating from university in 1991. I started my career working and living in Cologne, Germany, where I was fortunate to learn about German architects such as Ungers. The seriousness with which German architects design and how they pay such great attention to detailing and materializing their projects is truly astounding. The bold, competitive culture of the Germans was simply unknown in the Netherlands.

In 1993, I returned to the Netherlands and broadened my experience working at different architectural offices. In 2003, I made the bold move to start my own architecture studio, UArchitects. My first aim was not to name the studio after the architects, but to find a name that conveys the studio's main objectives: *Urban design and Architecture.*
I sincerely hope you enjoy reading this book on the projects that UArchitects has worked on, and certainly recommend visiting some of the projects if you have the time. This is a collection of building projects.

Remember to take your time to appreciate and learn about architecture and allocate less time to social media and the use of AI.

Misak Terzibasiyan, 2024

NEW OPPORTUNITY

"space and light"

The allurement in these kinds of projects are the client's unique wishes and budgets, the historical plan for visual quality plan, and the reintroduction of the concepts of spatiality, tactility.

All outside walls and the roof of the existing dwelling on the Dorpsstraat have been left intact, in line with the requirements to preserve its historical character. The home was originally made up of small, closed-off rooms that allowed very little daylight in and offered no view from the living room to the extended back garden.

To open up the home, the idea was to review the constraints and introduce a different kind of spatiality and tactility that could create direct connections and perceptions between the existing front room and the back garden through the new extension and the various new sequences.

That sense of spatiality has been brought to life from centrally within and seamlessly connects the existing and the new. The materialisation and colour scheme is designed so that this continuity is perceptible in the interior through different sightlines, openings, connections and the treatment of surfaces.

The stairs and built-in cupboards have been given the same finish as the connecting stairs in the intersection of the existing house and the new extension.

Thermally modified timber was chosen for the exterior.
The laths were accurately drawn with attention to detail, and fixed on to the rear structure using a newly researched fixation method that hides the fasteners from view. This creates a light and demountable system of exterior wooden slats, which can easily be replaced as elements in the future. The upper floor of the new building has been set up as a timber frame construction to enhance the perspective through the sloping surfaces and lines that accelerate towards each other.

"remodelled home "

An additional advantage of this system is the huge savings it has provided for the dimension of the foundation, ultimately eliminating the need for piles. This would have never been possible in a traditional construction method. Furthermore, the substructure of the extension/new building is a construction system that is lightweight using Poroton walls, with stucco as exterior cladding. The frames are made of wood and have a transparent lacquer finish.

The interior finishing consists of oiled French oak at the stairs and the hidden cupboards underneath the stairs. This creates a direction and relationship from the old building to the rear garden of the property. The interior concept has been completely redesigned in order to experience the connection and spaciousness between the old building and the new building every day through natural light, routing and materials.

KITCHEN
LIVING
NEW
OLD
LIVING
LIVING
TOILET
NEW
OLD
NEW
OLD

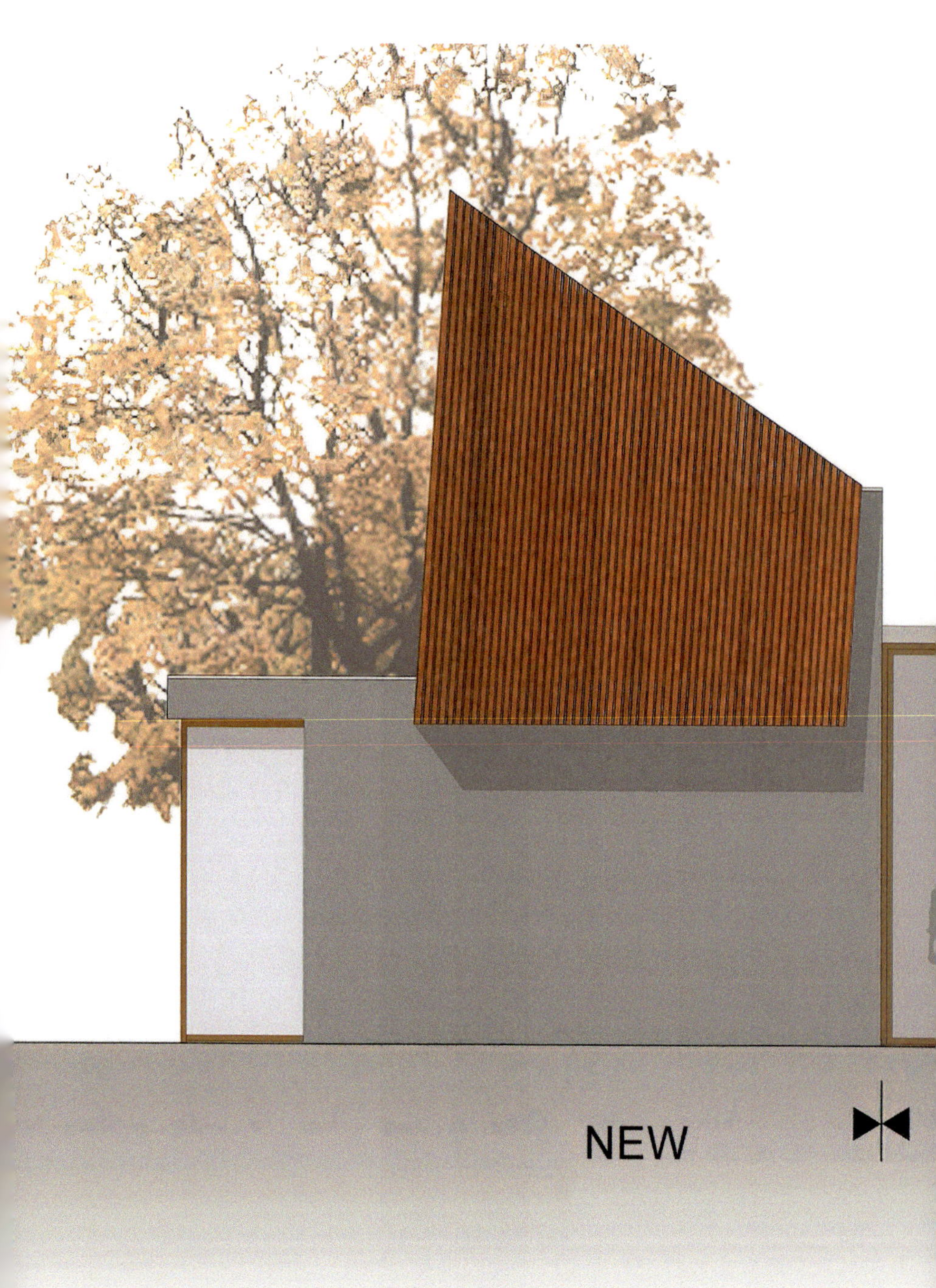

NEW

OLD

SALT STORAGE

"salt and ice"

To stay within the limitations of the request to design and install a straightforward roof, the idea was to express the identity and context of the Dutch Public Works and Water Management support point and, in doing so, to give meaning to this relatively nondescript spot on an industrial estate along a motorway somewhere in the Netherlands.

A metaphor of criss-crossing sheets of ice that slide over each other was sought to that end, a metaphor explaining the purpose of the support point as an operational winter road maintenance control centre.

The proposed concept provides an integral solution for the various programme components, including a de-icing salt storage facility and parking depot for snow ploughs and salt spreaders. The existing office and emergency depot will be retained.

The layout of the site is based on an industrial yard typology, arranging the various functions around a central open courtyard, all visible from the existing office to ensure a clear overview.

An important starting point for selecting the materials is taking account of the extremely corrosive environment associated with the salt yard's function. A modular pre-cast concrete element has been developed for the substructure, to compose a plinth that frames and demarcates the site.

The roof is presented as a dynamic structure that refers to creeping ice. The roof canopies over the robust concrete substructure and appears to float due to the pronounced contrast in shape and material.

The visual quality of the architecture is defined predominantly by the contrast between the two building components.

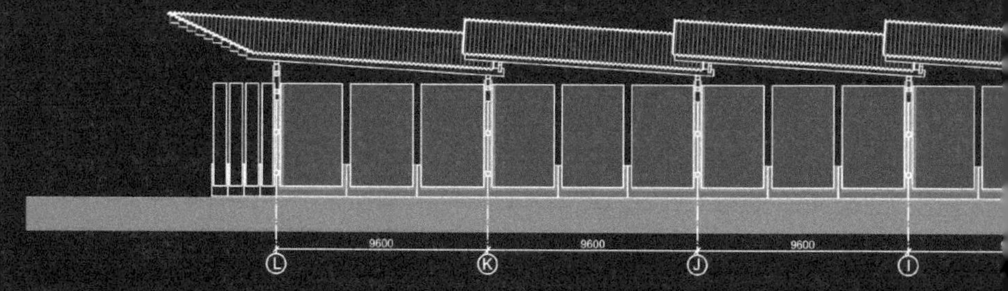

9600
9600
9600
L
K
J
I

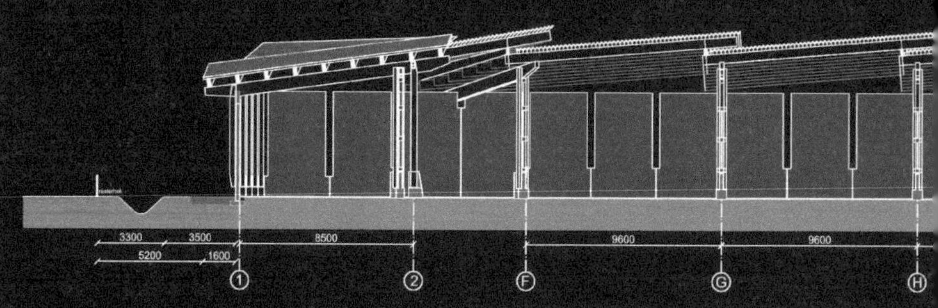

3300
3500
8500
9600
9600
5200
1600
1
2
F
G
H

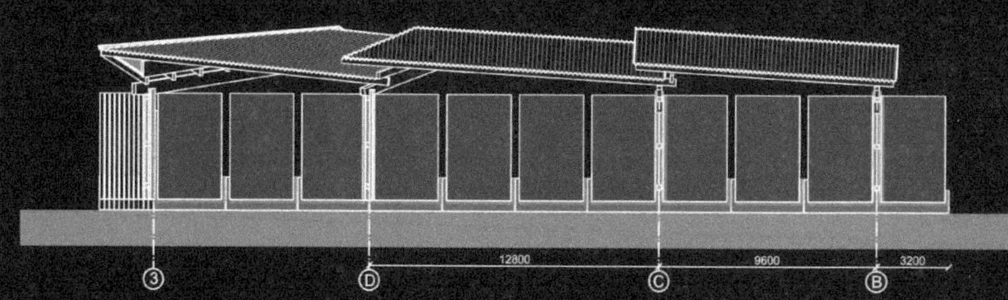

12800
9600
3200
3
D
C
B

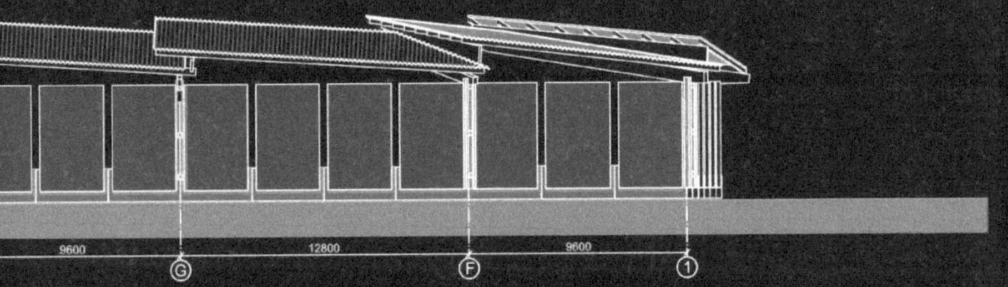

9600
12800
9600
G
F
1

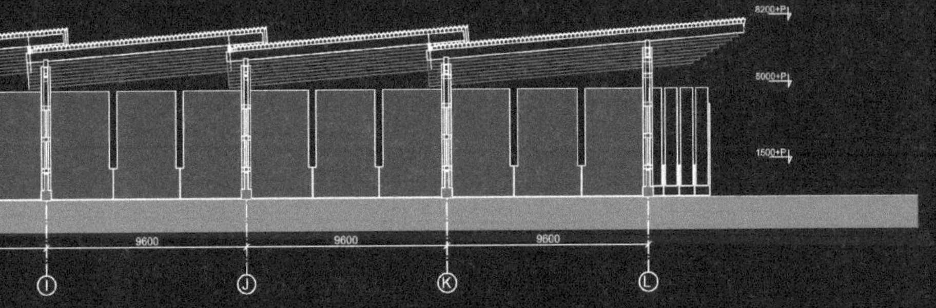

8200+P
5000+P
1500+P
9600
9600
9600
I
J
K
L

JUVENILE DETENTION PAVILION

"light and temporary"

Pavilion for visitors and education

Unit 5 of the "c" in Overloon is converted from an institution for adults into an autonomously functioning juvenile detention institution.

A new and more intensive interaction with the surrounding nature is aimed at for the youngsters.

The resoluteness of the world which aims at the interior is partly removed, so that the youngsters can prepare themselves for their return in society.

The concept aims at an open, transparent building between the closed prison and the outside world. Visitors can throw a glance at the prison life and the youngsters can look at the outside world, the society in which they will return later on.

For the flexibility at future changes in the program and treatment, the construction is situated in the side façade, the service pipes have been integrated centrally and the side façades are composed of front elements which can be changed modularly.

1 Entrance traffic
2 Living area
3 Pavilion for education and visitors
4 Living area
5 Entrance visitors

By means of the light appearance and the placement on metal feet in the woodland soil, the volume seems to float in the wood. Because of the layered façade in steel, aluminium and Bangkirai the building will be merged in the surrounding woodland scenery, showing different shades of grey.

The class-rooms on the first floor and the visiting rooms on the ground floor are functioning separately from each other by means of the two outside stairs in the head façades.

At the entrance to the visiting room there is a hall in which both functions are in contact with each other, dramatizing the moment of the meeting between the youngsters and the visitors.

The severe measures and the rhythmic of the carefully detailed elements of the façade may lend a structure to the youngsters, which they need to proceed their way.

This pavilion is the first phase of a masterplan.

Ground plan

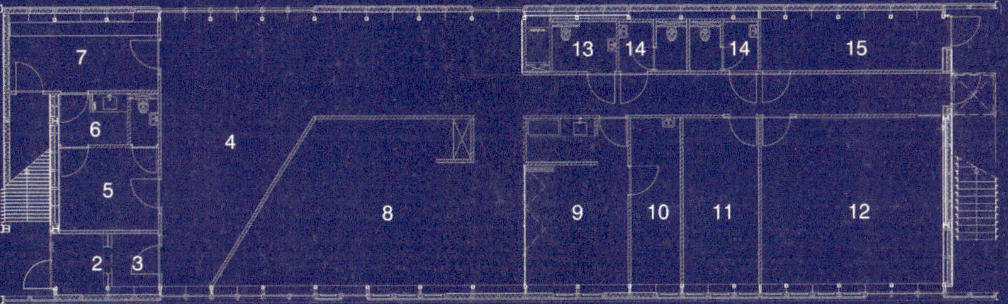

1 Entrance
2 Metal detector
3 Entrance hall
4 Waiting room visitors
5 Consultancy

6 Visitation
7 Waiting room / Consultancy
8 Visiting room / Library
9 Multi-religious centre
10 Storage room

11 Office
12 Meeting / Reading room
13 Toilet disabled
14 Toilet
15 Storage room

First floor

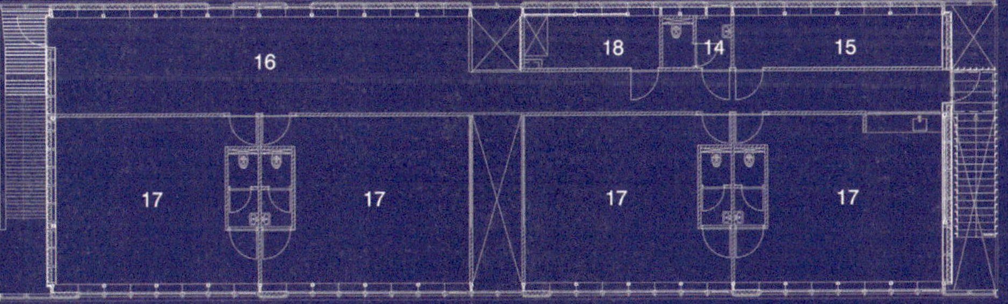

14 Toilet
15 Storage room
16 Corridor
17 Education
18 Installations

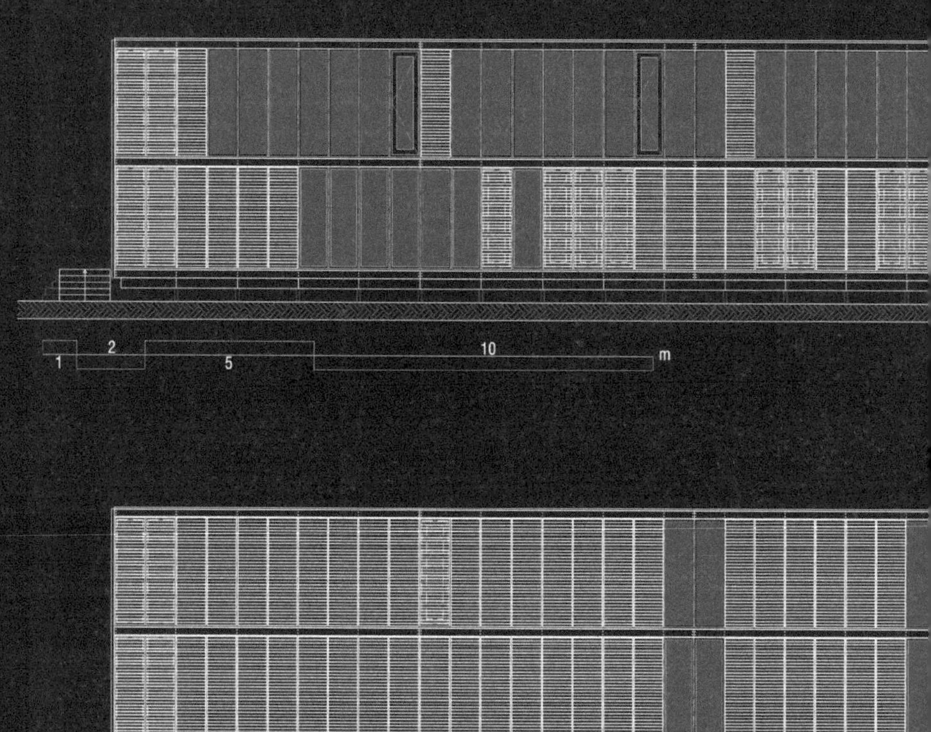

2
1
5
10
m
2
1
5
10
m

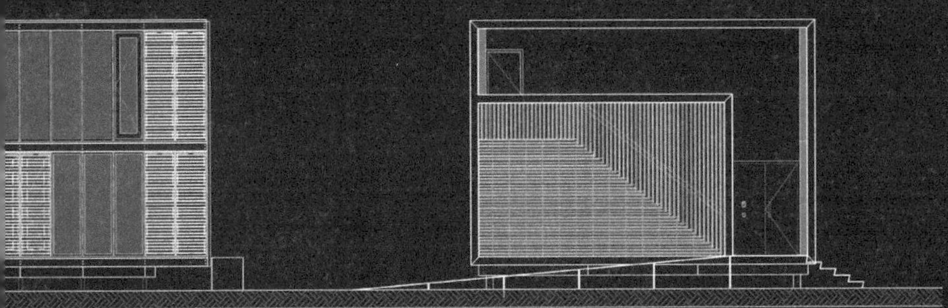

t elevation

South elevation

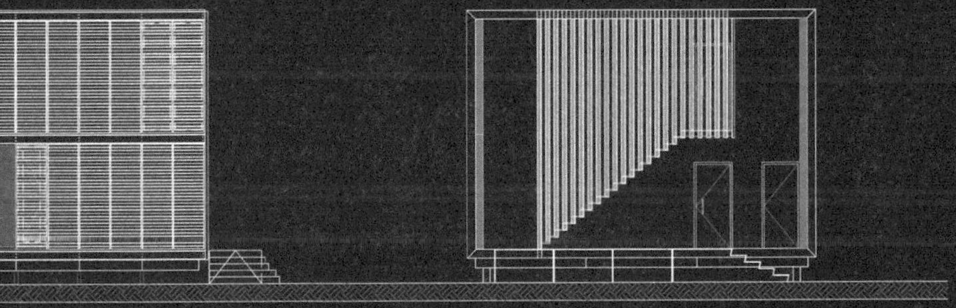

t elevation

North elevation

"time-out"

Unit 5 of "JJI De Hunnerberg, De Maasberg" in Overloon is converted from a prison for adults into an autonomously functioning juvenile detention institution. This is the first juvenile detention in the Netherlands where youngsters are treated in small groups of ten instead of twelve. So each youngster gets more treatment and coaching.

The old school is mainly demolished and partly renovated with the sports accommodation and a new building for the living area have been realised. This new building for living is the main part of the masterplan.

Concept

The resoluteness of the world which aims at the interior is partly removed. A new and more intensive interaction with the surrounding nature is aimed at for the youngsters. The open structure stimulates the daily shifts between living, learning and recreation.

Site and organisation

The new building for living is situated parallel to the regional public road and contains 4 sectors with 10 youngsters each. In the longitudinal direction the building is organized linearly with bedrooms on the street side with an open view. The team rooms have been placed in the centre.

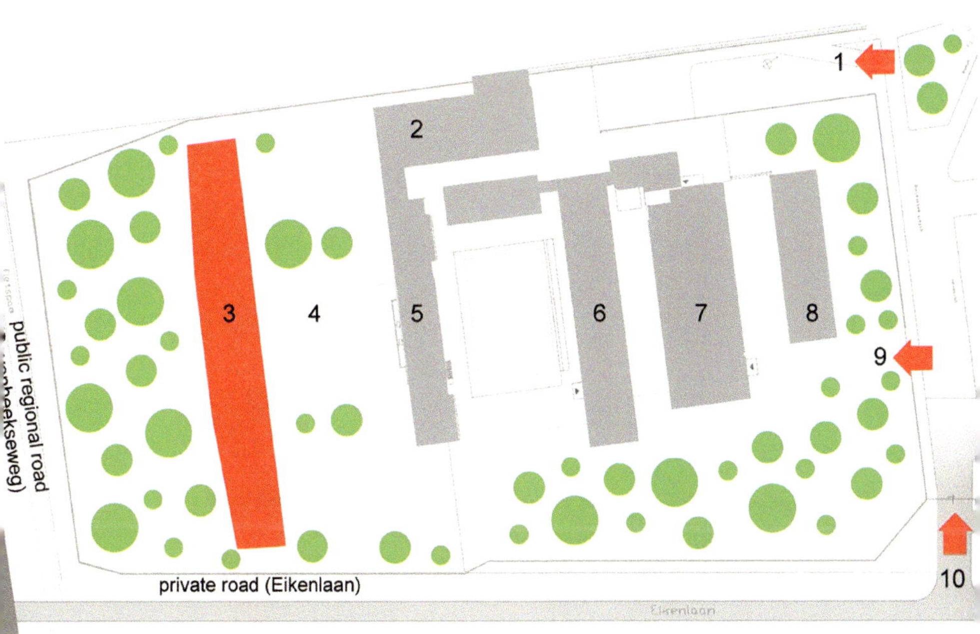

1 Entrance to area for transport
2 Renovation gymnasium
3 New building for living
4 Recreation outdoor
5 Renovation building for living
6 Existing building for living
7 Existing building for workplaces and treatment
8 Pavillion for education and visitors
9 Entrance to area for pedestrians and visitors
10 Main entrance

Facades

Some youngsters are staying in this building because they are themselves victim
of lover boys or incest. Other youngsters are placed for means of punishment.
The building for living area should provide the youngsters a place for protection.
It is a temporarily home base for the youngsters. The façade of this home base is
constructed with big dark-grey bricks (dimensions 290 x 195 x 90 mm), which express
the solid social resistance.

The façade towards the street shows an abstract pattern of brickwork with vertical
glass openings. Two enormous (maximum glass dimensions) glass openings are
contrasting with this mainly closed façade and reveal the communal living rooms.

The building opens up to the other side with the enclosed outdoor spaces. Wooden
facades and concrete planes reveal the atmosphere of the interior.
The circular element on the south works on the urban scale as a turning point and it
shows the entrance.

(Im)perfection and texture

The vertical pattern of the glass openings are inspired by the rhythm of the
surrounding trees.

 Each sleeping room is unique, just like each youngster is unique. This is emphasized
by the different colors in the interior and the different windows. The vertical
apertures have different bevel edges allowing the youngsters to have different sight
lines to the surrounding wood land scenery.

We had the idea that the stones should not be too smooth and shiny. That would not
match with the texture of the surroundings and the youngsters. So we selected a
brick with a the texture that has small vertical cuts and is relatively dark.

Prefabrication

4200 stones are sliced and with different angles glued together to prefabricate the corner-stones with different angles. In this way the thickness is not visible from outside, which emphasizes the solid character of the building. There are no vertical masonry joints, which leads to small vertical lines of shadow between the stones. The dilatations are also invisible.

Relation youngster - environment

The measurement of the bricks is balancing with the subtle way how the spatial context and landscape is expressed in the building. Maybe the youngsters can find a new structure, which they need to proceed their way.

The texture and dimensions of the stone perfectly express the social (youngsters) and physical (woodland) context of the building.

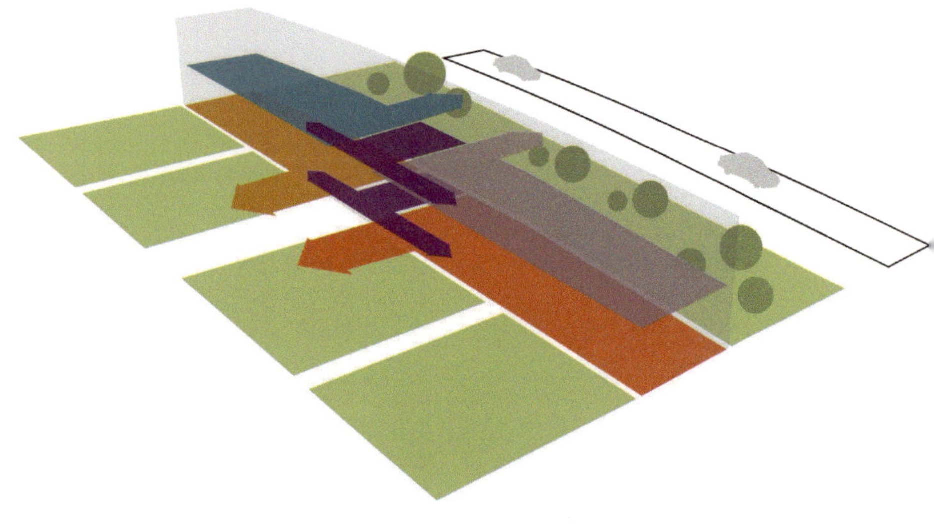

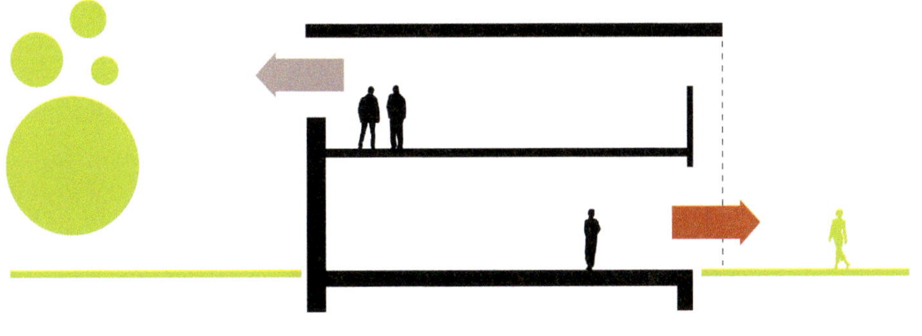

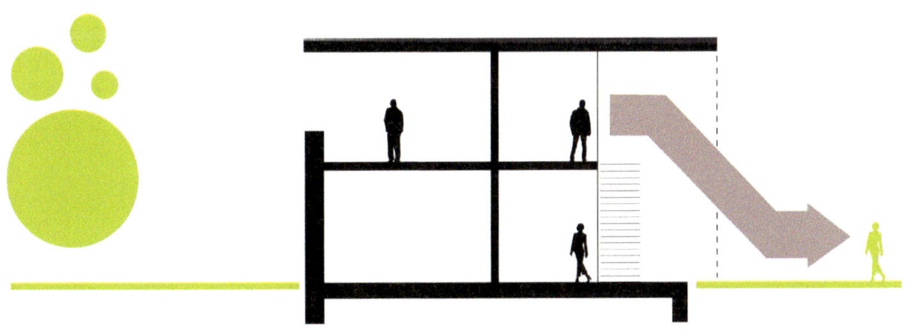

"split view"

This family which wanted to build this house was motivated by the change of their living situation and wanted to express this also in their new house. The two children of this family wanted to have their own living surrounding but also wanted to be in close contact with the parents. On the other hand the parents wanted to have more private zones in the new house but also be in close contact with their children.

Every floor of the house had to have an overview of the surrounding. In a certain way the new house is a translation of the family situation which is undergoing a transformation like many other families in the Netherlands.

The physical vision: *tree concept of living.*

The family wanted a house which is flooded with light, which is experienced each season in a different way and they wanted to experience the surrounding from different locations in the house.

To live is like to live in a tree with different levels, the core of the tree is the staircase. From the outside this house gives a readable split level. A glimpse of the various functions of the house can been seen at different corners from outside and inside the house.

The social vision: the way we live in spaces and remember.

For the term "split view" we could also use the term split mind, because the memory of the users of an average traditional house is at its best in traditional closed spaces (book of Joshua Foer). This theme mentioned in the book of Joshua Foer is as followed: If the person leaves the space where he has learned or read, the thought is easily forgotten by leaving the closed space and when the person returns to the same space, then this person remembers again the thought in question.

Our mind/memory is categorized in rooms/spaces.

This house will be an interesting thought and behaviour experiment because here are various crossover and open connections between different spaces. We question ourselves which effect this split view house will have on the mind and the remembering of facts and thoughts of the users of this house and will it result in a split mind/memory which is a modern variant is of our modern time of remembering and acting in this rapidly changing and liquid society. Will the task of remembering and acting be influenced by the see-through and open connections in this split view house ? The interior of this house and the use is readable at the outside of the house and each side of the house is reacting in his own peculiar way, one time closed and the other time open, sometimes friendly and the other time hard-minded, sometimes unanswered and the other time it lights up and shows the inside. All the sides of the house have a different expression in an abstract way.

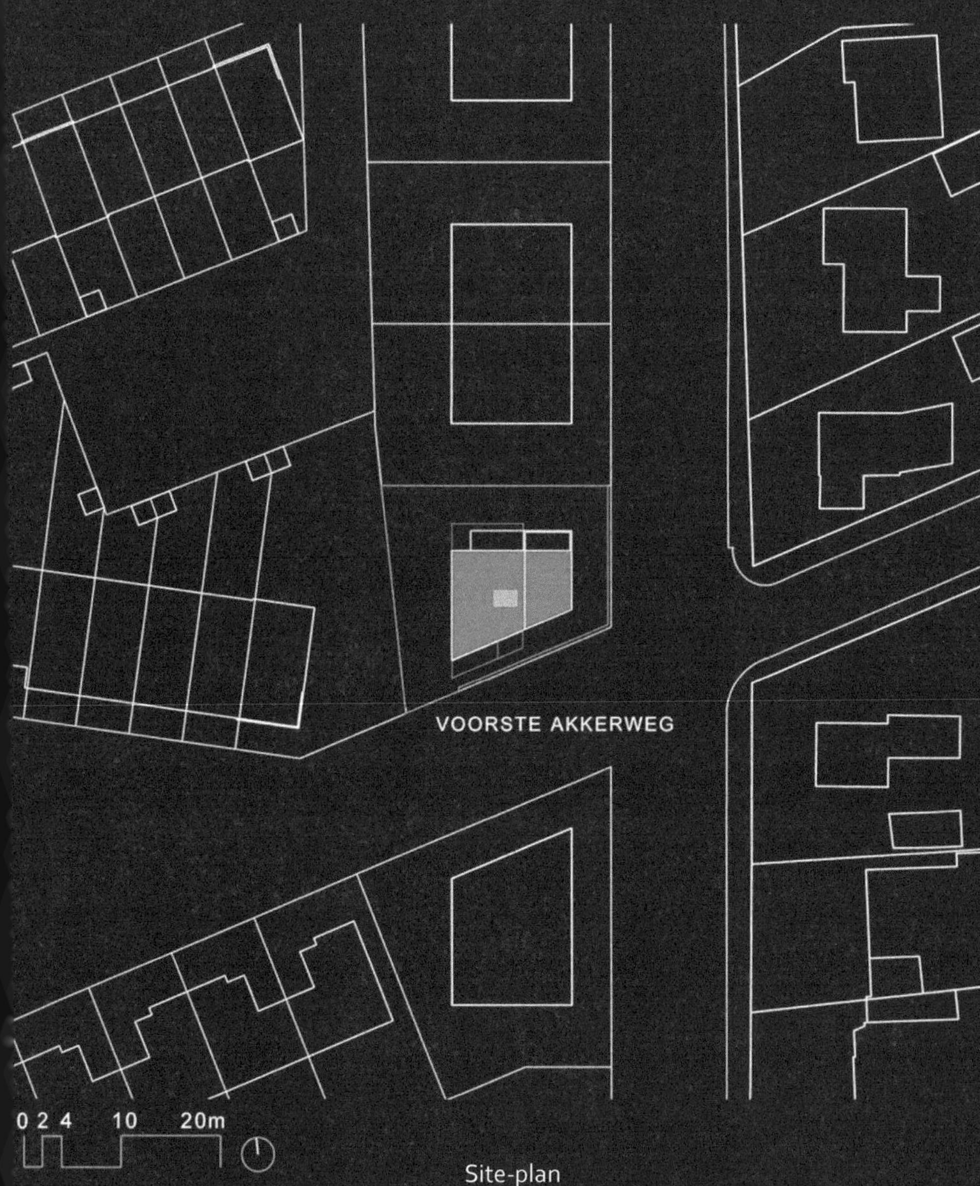

Site-plan

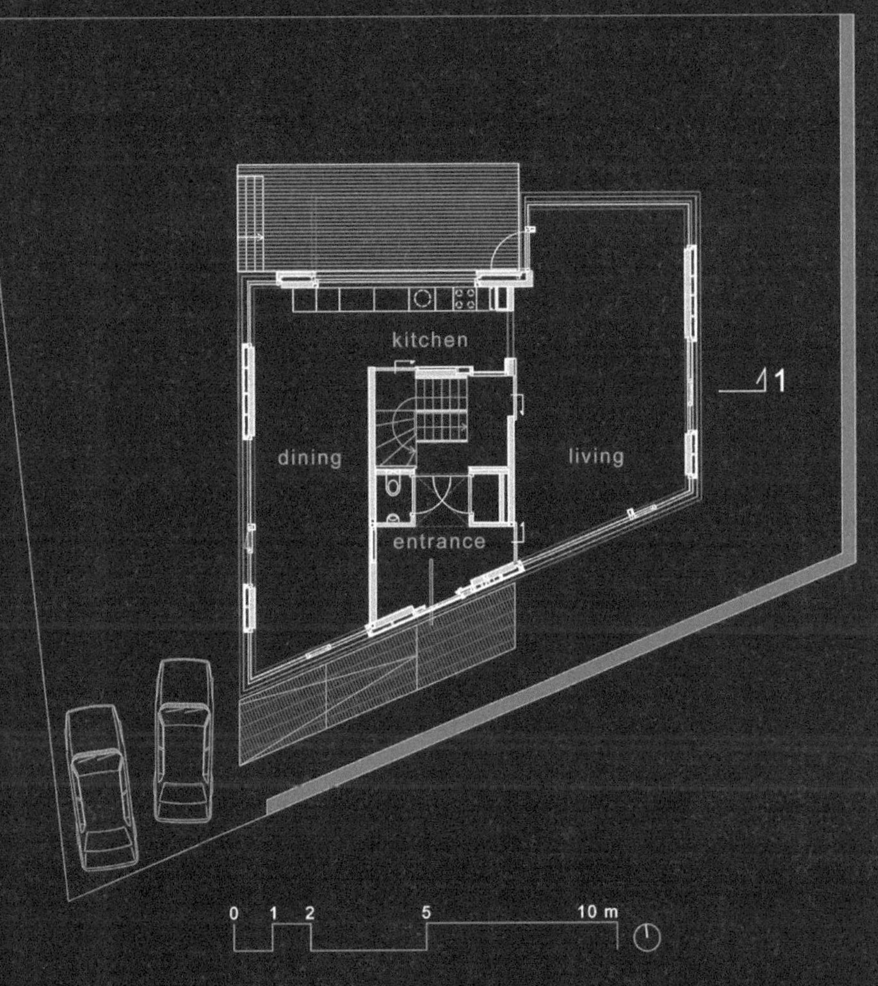

Ground floor

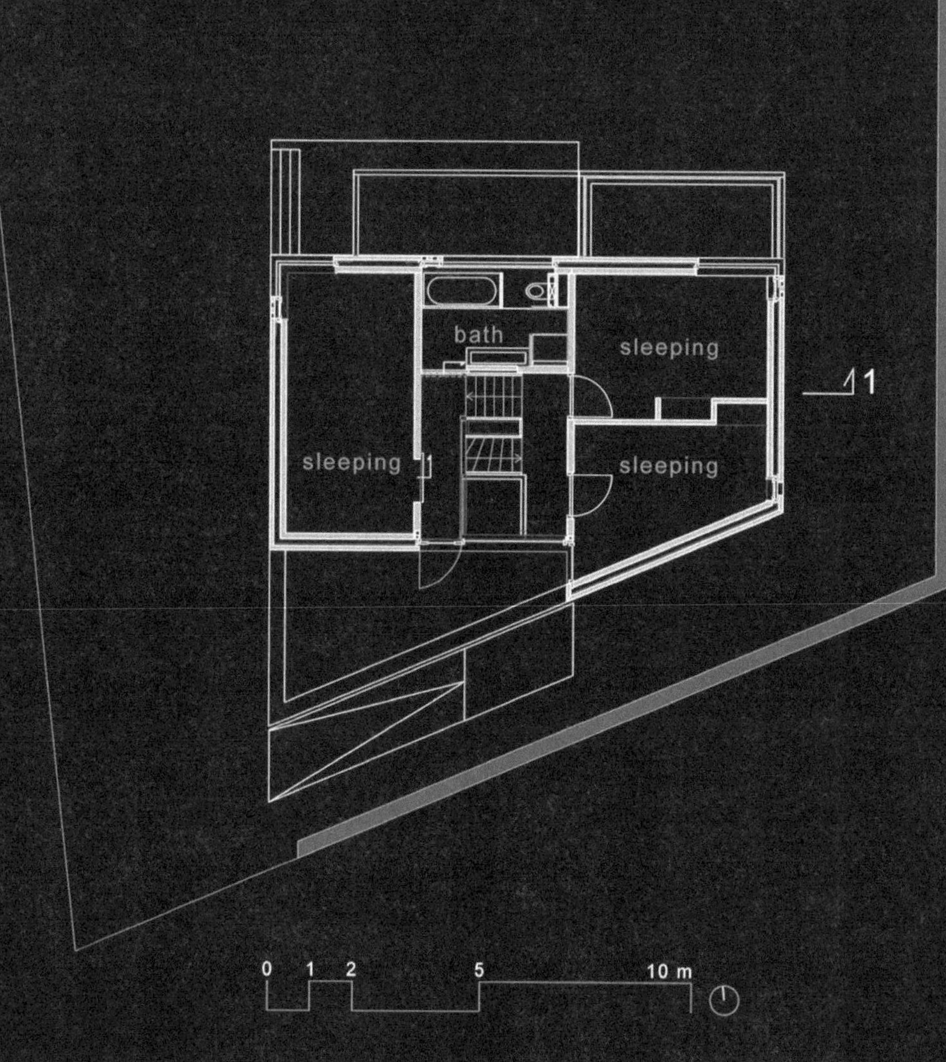

First floor

Main question

What does a building look like that is closed during the winter and is only open during the summer season?

The different seasons are noticeable in the appearance of the building. In the winter, the building is uninhabited and it appears to be a closed and therefore becomes an inanimate object. But when the sun comes out again, the summer is welcomed and the entire buildings appearance changes; the screens pop up, the facades slide open and the flags soar high in the sky. The summer sun opens the building to the world.

The appearance of the building is determined by the passing seasons.

Context

The lifeguard office is on the border between land and water.

The lower position of the building in comparison to the boulevard is imitated in the facade with a horizontal divide: the ground floor forms a robust plinth which makes a subtle connection to the beach with its light yellow-grey colour. The first floor is open, transparent and light weight. From the boulevard the transition between these two materials is exactly at eye level; as if the wooden superstructure could be floating on the water. The transition of the materials reinforces this illusion of the perspective.

The view is essential for a safe beach community. One side faces the water for the lifeguards and the other side faces the boulevard in front of the police station. The building is situated at the ramp to the beach.

Functional

The desire for a functional building is always important, but plays an even greater role in the function of a lifeguard office: in an emergency, every second counts.

The basic shape is a rectangle, with the viewing terrace facing outwards towards the water. The streamlined staircase is next to a fast access route to the lifeboat in the event of an emergency. The other side of the building provides space for a police station to receive visitors and prepare an official report. The ground floor is used for toilets for beach visitors, a first aid room and the storage room for the lifeboat.

Texture

Such a small building is ideal for experimenting with texture, colour and detail. Which allows you to create a unique solution, just like a tailor-made suit. Inspiration for the texture of the building has been found throughout the beach and in the filtering of light.

The concrete has been specially coloured with a light colour of yellow pigment. The grey colour of the concrete is therefore softened and a connection is established with the colour of the sand.

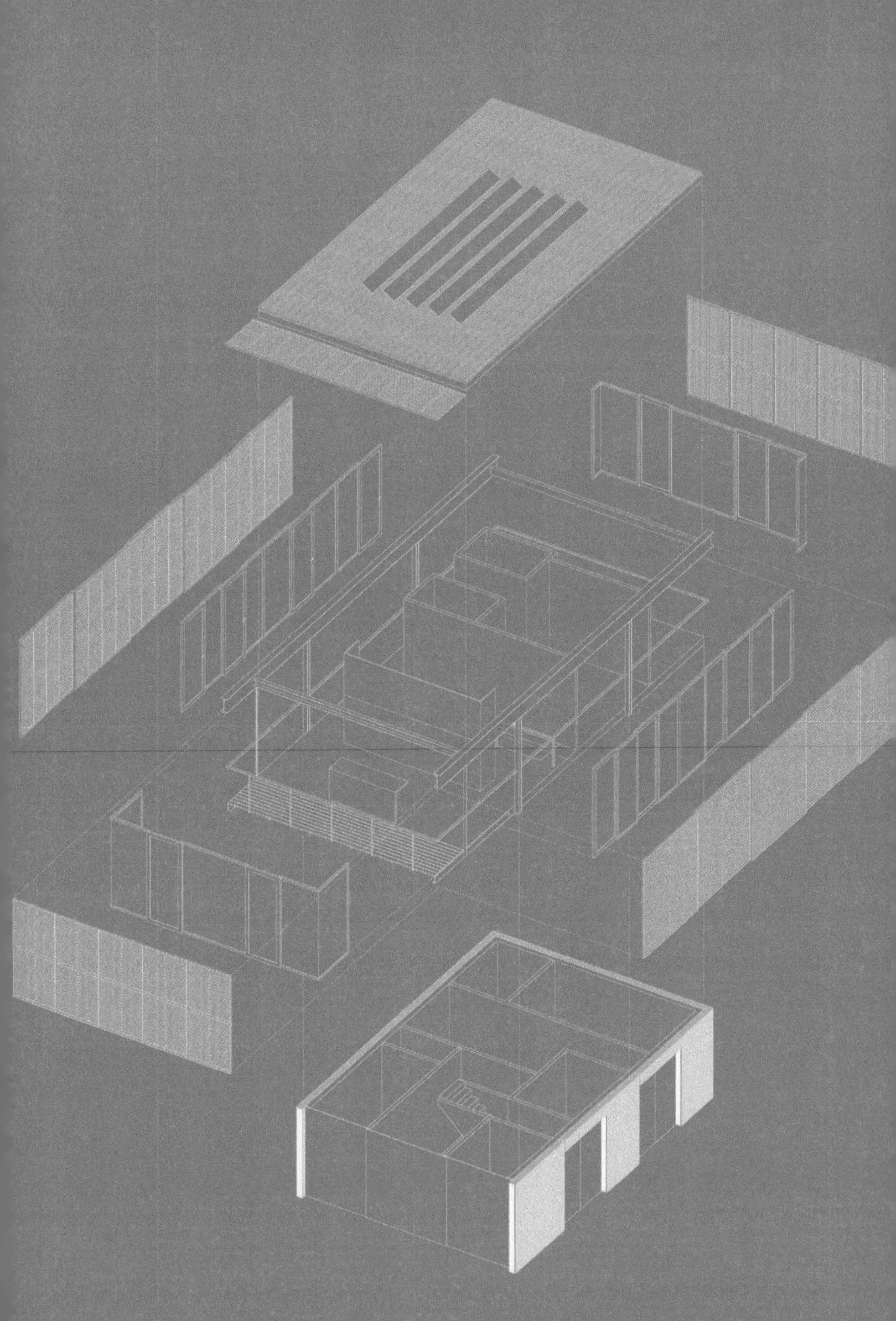

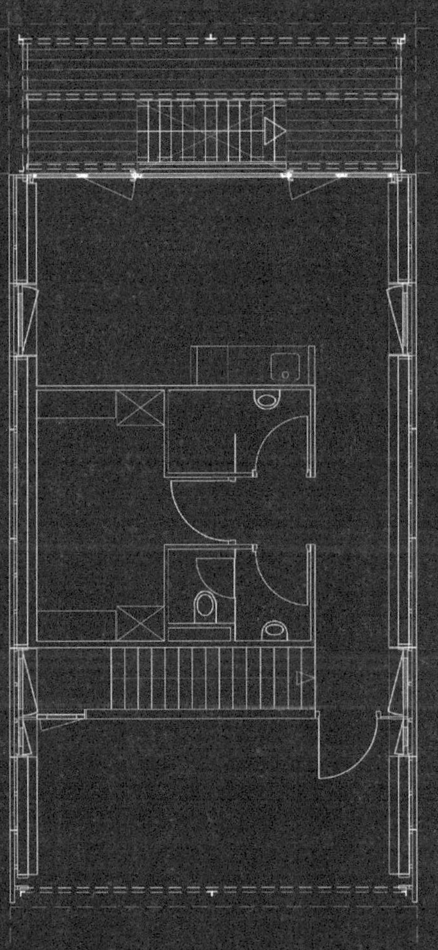

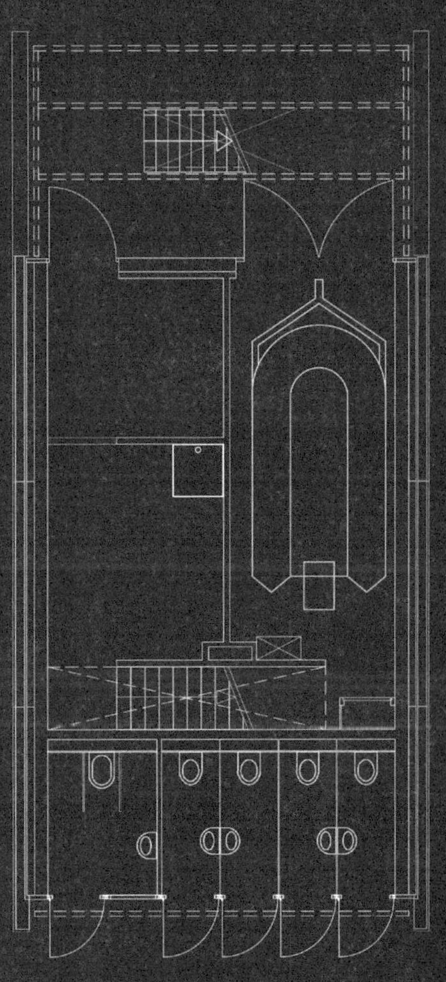

SCHOOL 'T HOFKE

This is a special primary school because there are 5 different groups of users who work together in one building, and use the facilities together for education, care, sports and neighborhood facilities. It consists of 16 classrooms, 3 groups for a daycare, 1 group for extra-curricular activities, 1 nursery school/kindergarten and one gym. The building has a social connection to the neighbourhood and also has rooms available for associations that want to use the extra consultation and meeting rooms.

Starting in 2006, in total this project took 6.5 years for our firm to prepare, including an interim suspension by the local authorities and ultimately with the construction work taking 1.5 years. The project is characterized by a number of important preconditions for which intensive and lengthy consultations were required, in order to reach agreement and consensus with all the interested parties in the neighborhood.

When we won the project at the end of 2005 after being in competition with other architectural firms, it was on the basis of our proposal in which the existing school would be maintained, renovated and partly extended with a new build.

As architects we made a strong case for our proposal, but during the design process over the years, it turned out that it would not be feasible due to a number of significant practical concerns: the strict preconditions for a protected green area located to the north of the site, the number of parking spaces (41) which had to be included and had to be above ground. In 2009 we restarted at our own initiative.

In the current project we looked for a connection to the old school, because people living around the school also intrinsically valued the previous school.

The white colour of the brick façades in this project is a direct reference to the same color of the previous school. The bricks were laid vertically in order to approach the tree bark (texture) effect of the monumental trees which also influenced the design process.

The texture and color of the facade refer to and connect to the context. The bricks are produced in the vicinity of the site in order to reduce the effects on the environment, so that no bricks are imported from another region or country.

The spatial core/open space of the building in the middle of the school is derived from the existing school and also forms the link where the school's different users meet. This is literally the connection between the left and right side of users and the core of the building contains the flexible spaces for general use.

We also ensured in the planning that several monumental trees are an integral part of the site plan we designed. Lines of the facade elements of the previous school are recalled in the lines of the playground paving.

Protection trees
(natural texture)

Wooden fence
(protected green area)

New school
(inspiration texture)

Protected trees
(natural texture)

Former school
(white color)

New school
(inspiration texture)

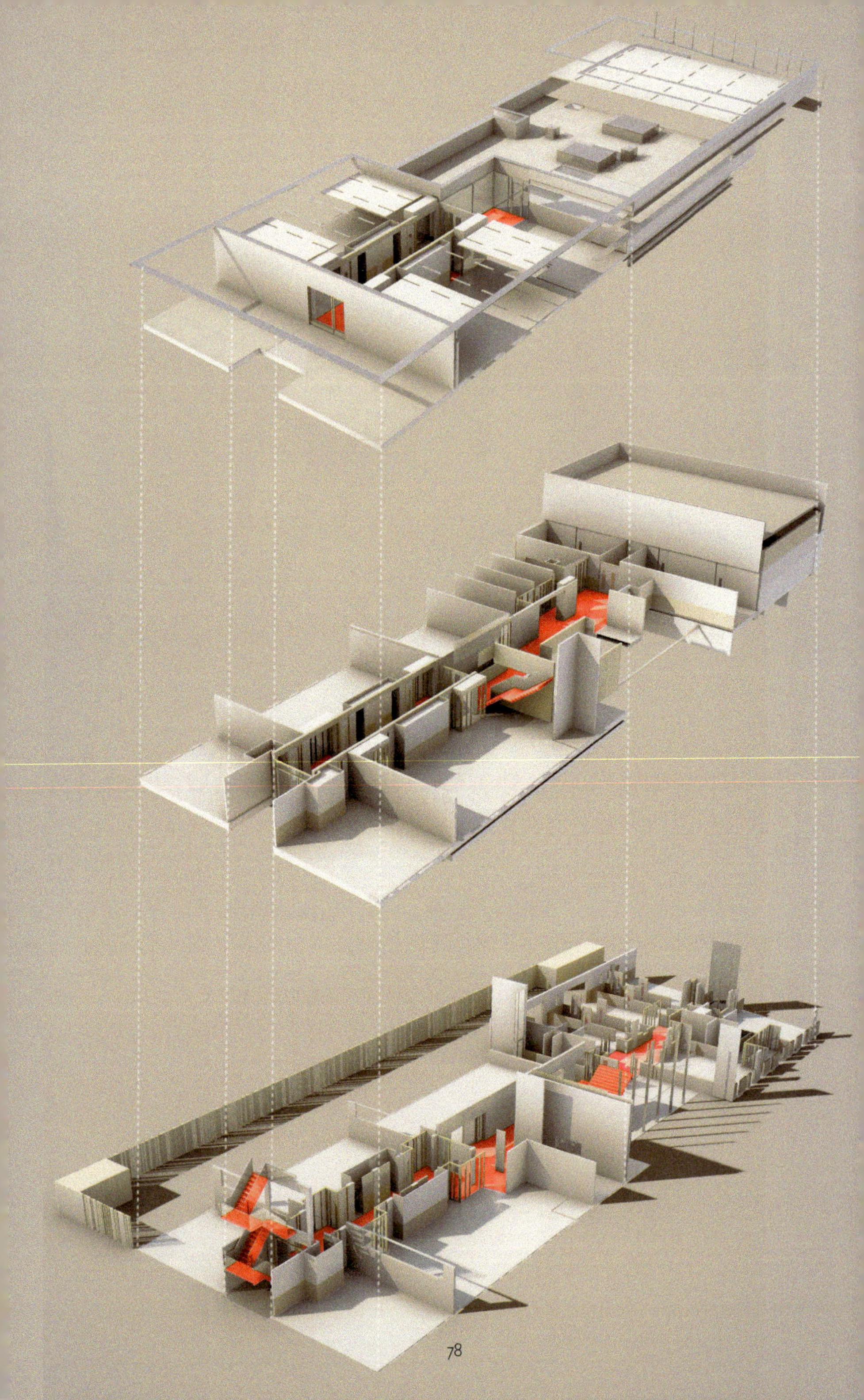

Ground plan

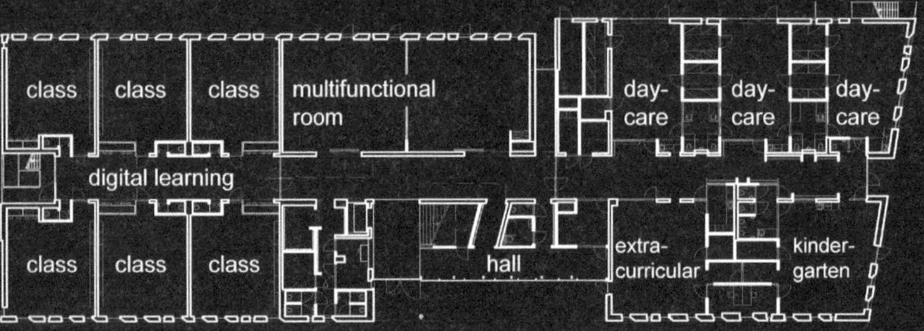

First floor

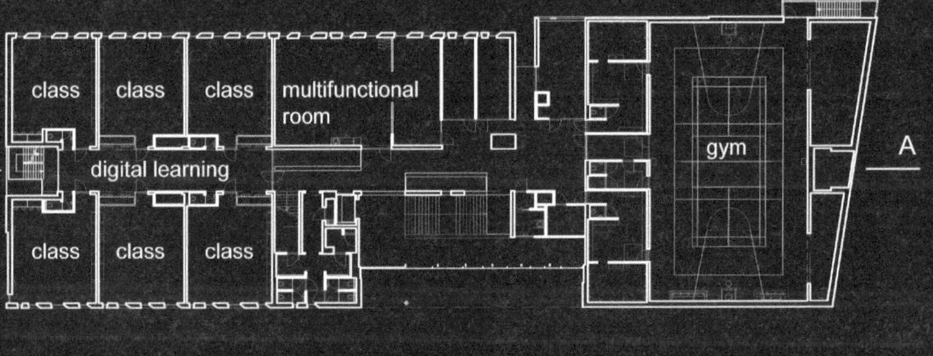

Section AA

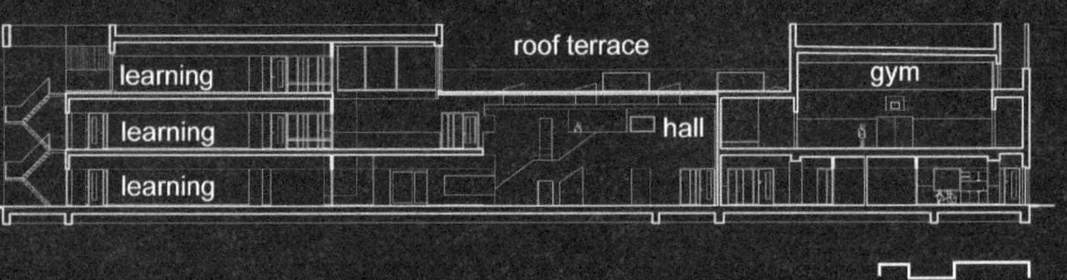

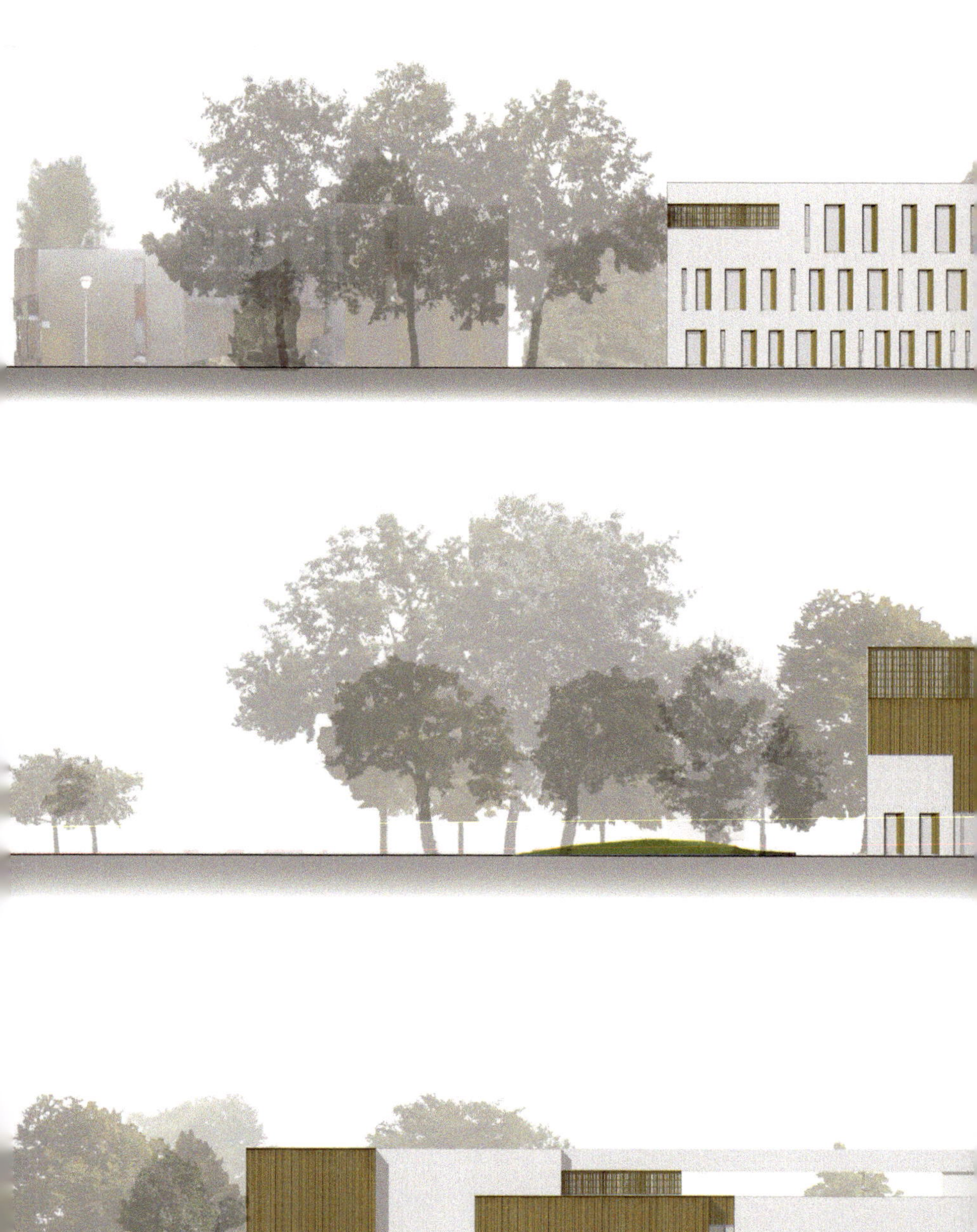

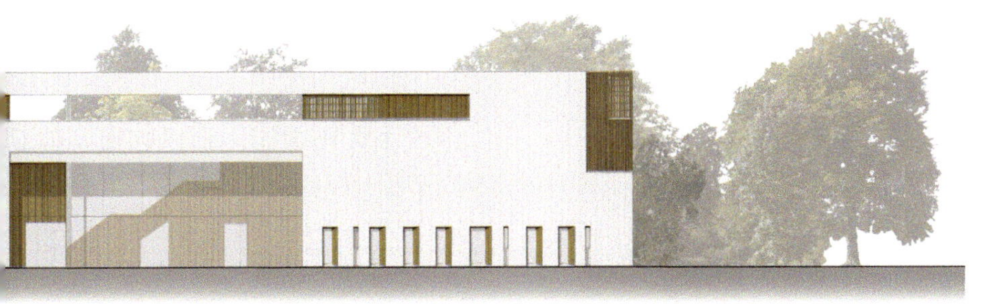

SCHOOL DE TWEESPRONG

De Tweesprong; NEW background for OLD school

The context is a small village in the southern half of the Netherlands. The existing building is situated in the small centre of the village diagonally opposite a Catholic church. The spatial relationship with the church creates a strong dialogue between the two public buildings, which were originally designed by the same architect. This project's aim was twofold: to take an existing part of the school back into use, and to extend the building with a new wing.

The existing part of the school is a symmetric construction featuring a painting by a well- known artist from this region. The villagers have a strong emotional attachment to this school.

The new corridor serves as an extension piece, encouraging children to learn outside the classroom and to play. A small library, a kindergarten and day-care centre reinforce the pivotal role played by the school in village life. It has become the new centre for children and adults alike.

The outside part of the new school has been designed with respect for the existing building (monumental building) The school opens out towards the north with a fascinating glass façade. This new façade is like a glass mirror that reflects the old school and the monumental old trees.

The roof of the new school is sloped at exactly the same angle as that of the old school. It is purposefully south-facing for the incorporation of solar PV panels, ensuring that the sun's rays are captured perfectly. Thick insulation retains warmth inside the building. The heat recovery system requires zero external energy through the reuse of heat/warmth.

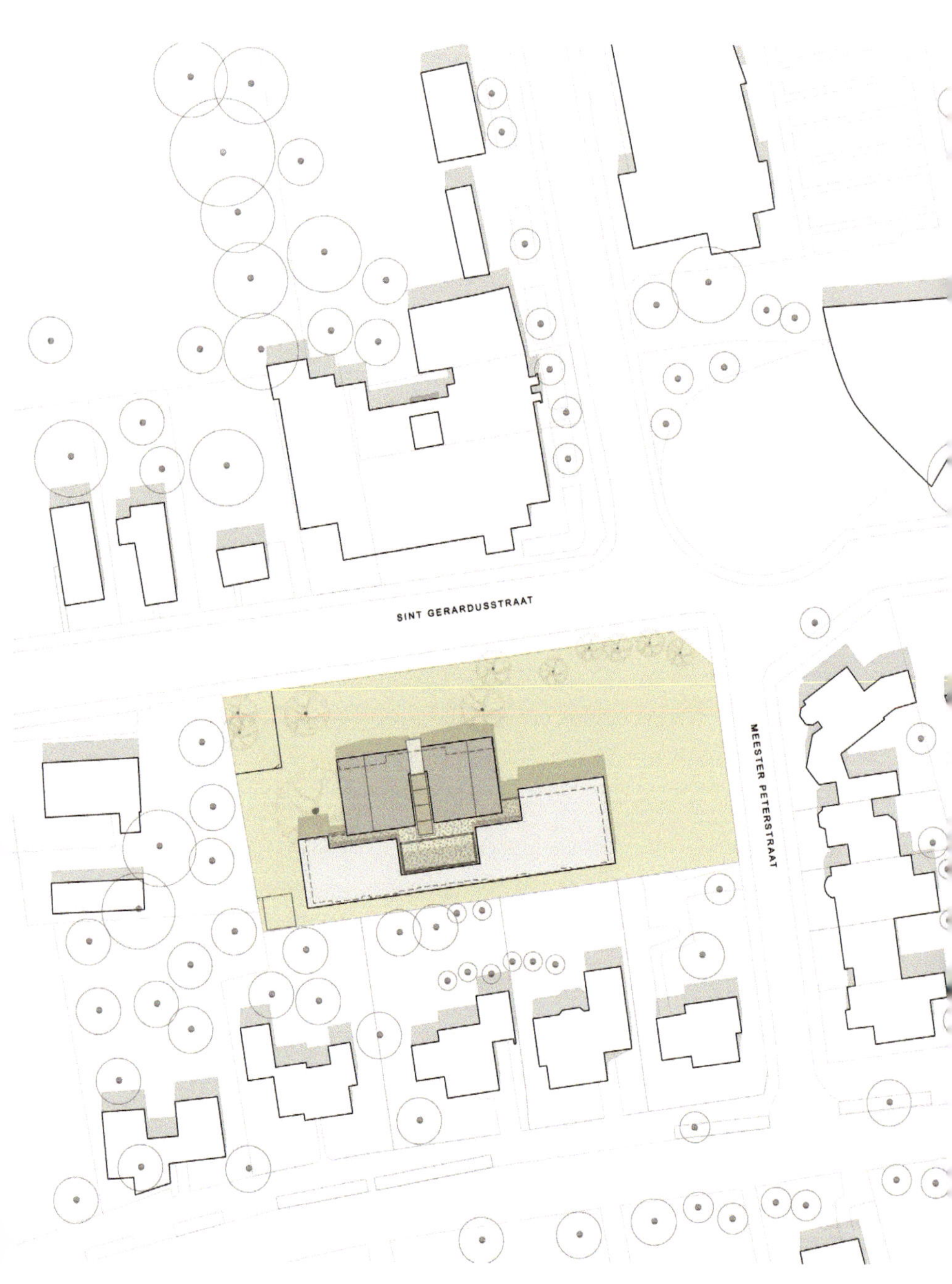

SINT GERARDUSSTRAAT
MEESTER PETERSTRAAT

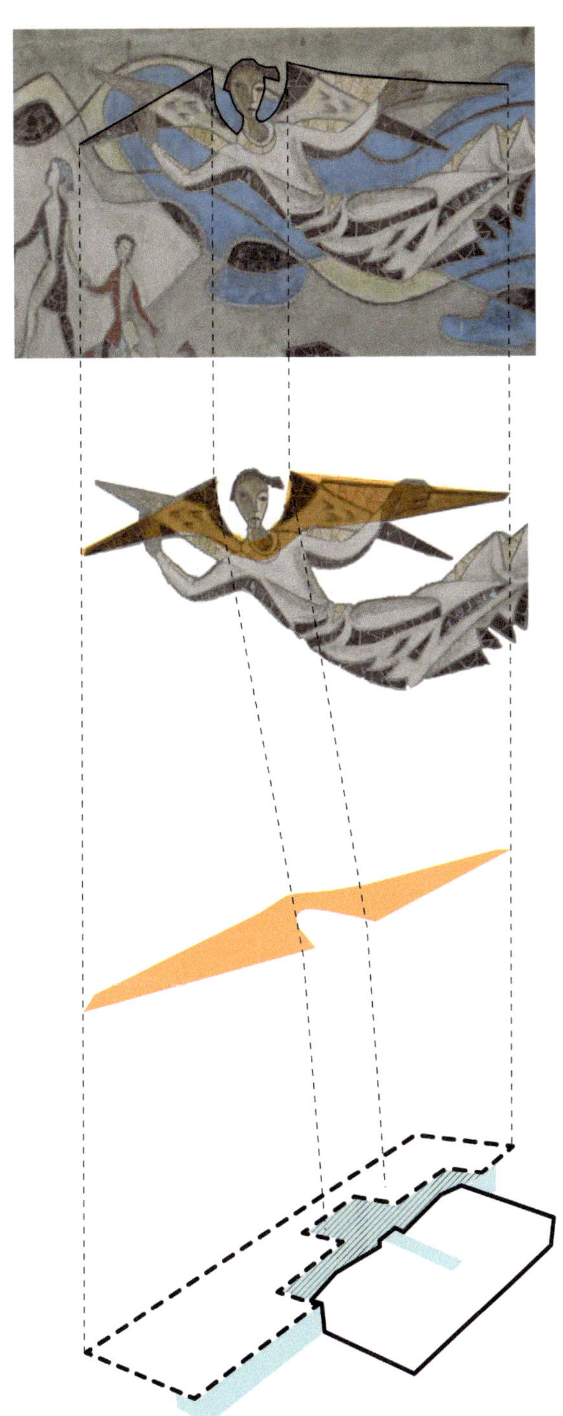

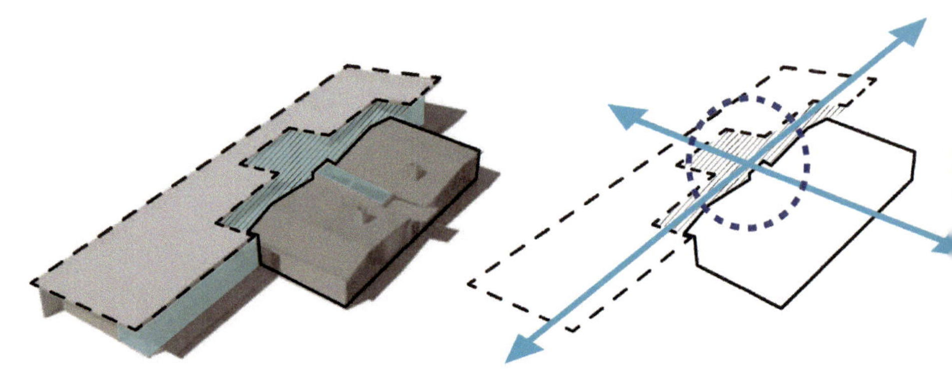

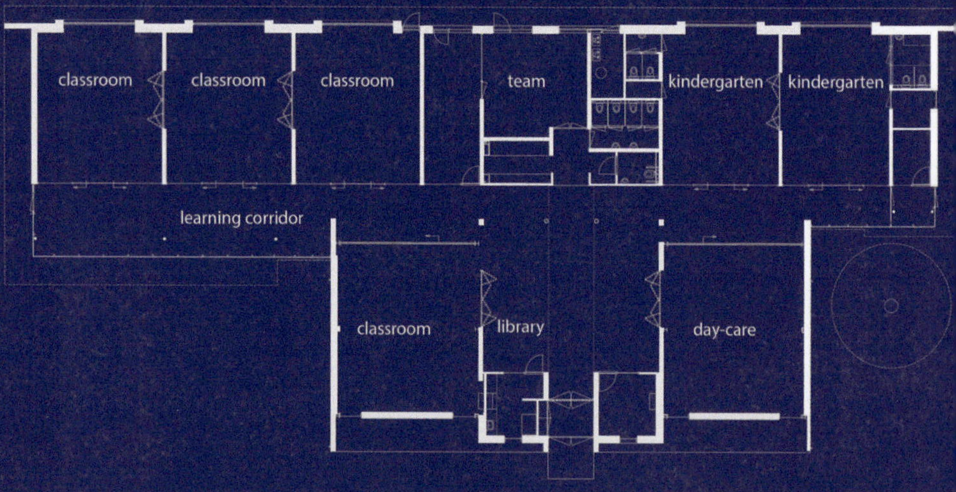

classroom
classroom
classroom
team
kindergarten
kindergarten
learning corridor
classroom
library
day-care

Zaanstad Sports Centre

The new Zaanstad-Zuid sports centre building has been built in the Poelenburg district next to the street De Weer. The urban development between the green area on De Weer street and the water alongside the M.L. Kingweg alternates between enclosed blocks of houses and businesses and a more open arrangement of school buildings and a religious centre.

During the day, the sports hall is used by these schools and it is subdivided into three areas. The students use the day entrance which opens directly into the playground. In the evenings and at the weekends the sports hall is used by sports associations and neighborhood groups who make use of the cafeteria area, the conference room, and the spectator stands which can hold 300 people. The evening entrance is on the other side of the building on De Weer street.

The change in use between day and evening is the basis of the concept. The routes from the side entrance in the playground and the route from the main entrance on De Weer street are the basis of the spatial structure.

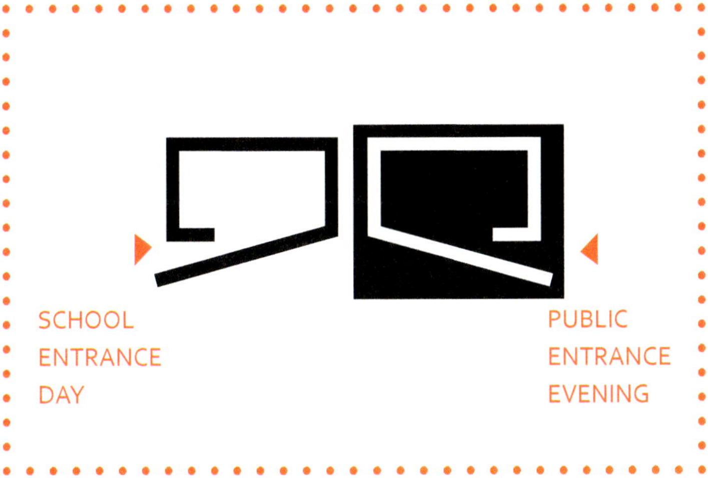

SCHOOL
ENTRANCE
DAY

PUBLIC
ENTRANCE
EVENING

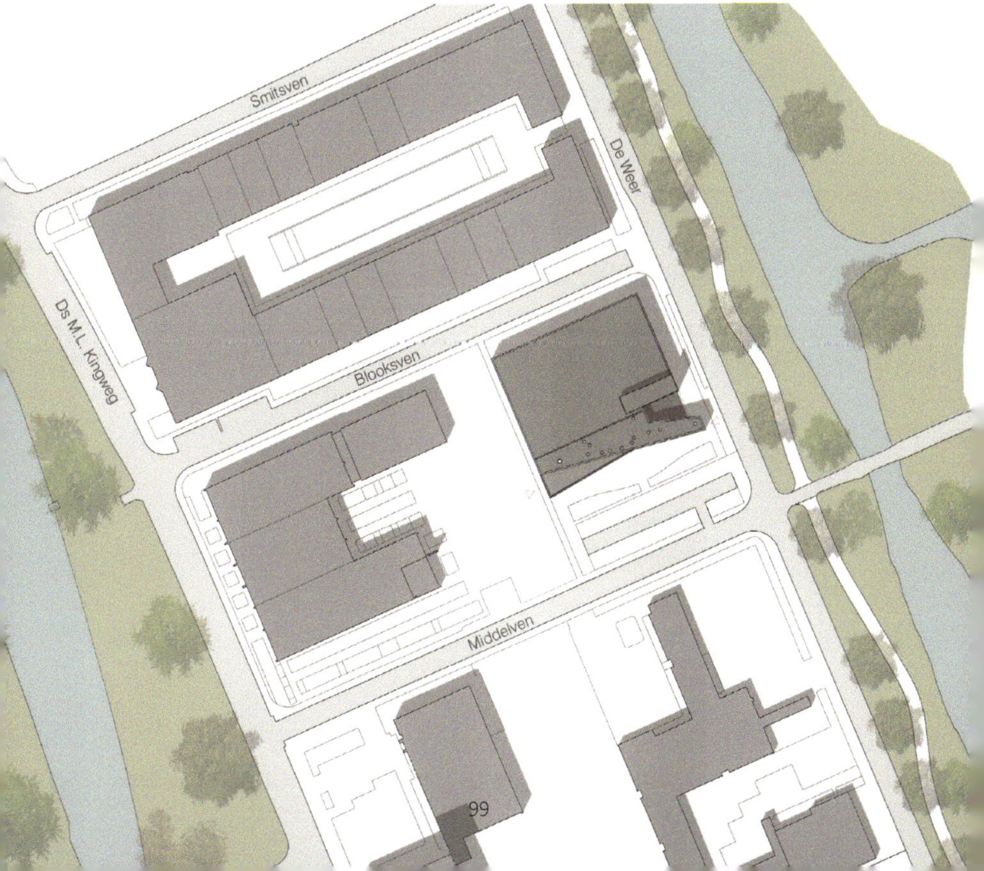

Smitsven
De Weer
Ds M.L. Kingweg
Blooksven
Middelven

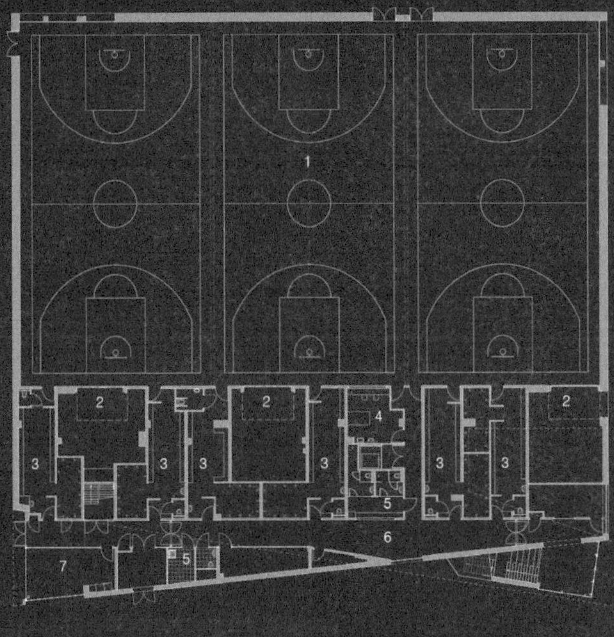

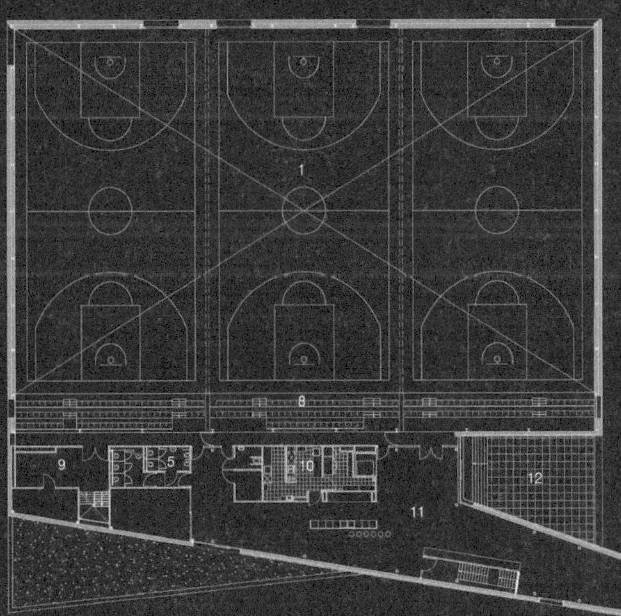

1 Sports hall
2 Storage
3 Dressing room
4 Referee and first aid
5 Dressing room for referee
   and teachers
6 Corridor
7 Teachers room
8 Spectators
9 Staircase
10 Kitchen
11 Cafetaria
12 Roof terrace

ZAAN

IKC DE GELUKSVOGEL

This a unique sustainable and digital school in the Netherlands.

Two existing schools in two neighbouring locations in Maastricht are merging into a new school on a new location in that city. This particular location was chosen to strengthen the weak social structure of the two neighbourhoods and to introduce a new digital education system to learn also more about the environment, nature and sustainability. Even the playground outside has different zones to help children (re) discover nature and explore their world by means of experiments or to build and test objects.

The digital way of teaching is for the most part paperless (virtual), which is represented in the architecture of the building. It shows a brick element with random messages in binary code (1 and 0) on the façade, as a reflection of this digitalized education system and the virtual reality in which we live today. The façade acts as the messenger of our digital world. Not in a direct, obvious way but more indirect, by the irregular placing of the bricks in patterns.

Both the school and the building are not designed around a classically organized educational system but around the concept of free movement and free use of spaces. We used the concept of a flock of birds to predict the movement of the users (children) through the building, which is how we designed the various spaces in the school. The educational space in the school is not limited to the classrooms but can continue in different open spaces with a different purpose. This open plan will encourage the free flow between and use of the spaces; education will not be limited by walls or doors. It even continues outside to the playground and the terraces on the first floor.

Together with the consultants, the building was designed to be flexible and adjustable. This means that if this building should get another function in the future, the different compartments that is made up of can easily be adjusted to the needs and wishes of another user, without losing its quality. The educational system and lessons are completely digital and are connected to the sports facilities and activities. The sports activities of the children can therefore be incorporated into the digital learning program.

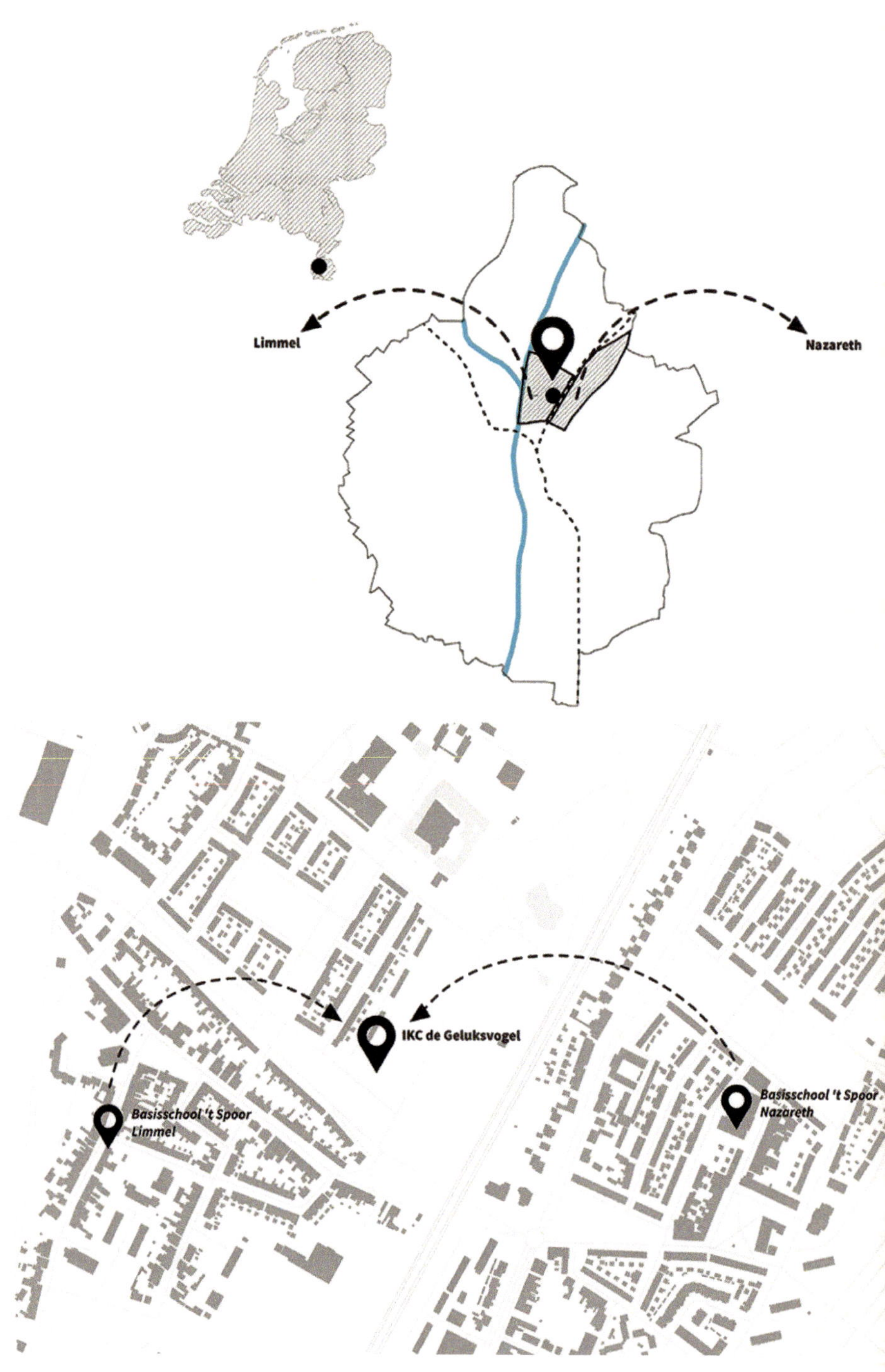
Limmel
Nazareth
IKC de Geluksvogel
Basisschool 't Spoor
Limmel
Basisschool 't Spoor
Nazareth

Digital society
binary language

```
010100100100100111010010100010010
010001010010011110001001010010001
000101110001100101010101011001010
100101010101010101010010101010101 0
101010101010101010110101010101010 1
010101010101010101010101010101010 1 0
101010111010101010101010110001011
000101010101010101010101010101010 1
010101001001010101001001011010010
```

Green existence
nature texture

Green society
binary language

```
0101001001001001110
1001010001001001000
1010010011110001001
0100100010001011100
0111001010101011100
```

Classical school

Swarm organisation

Swarm school

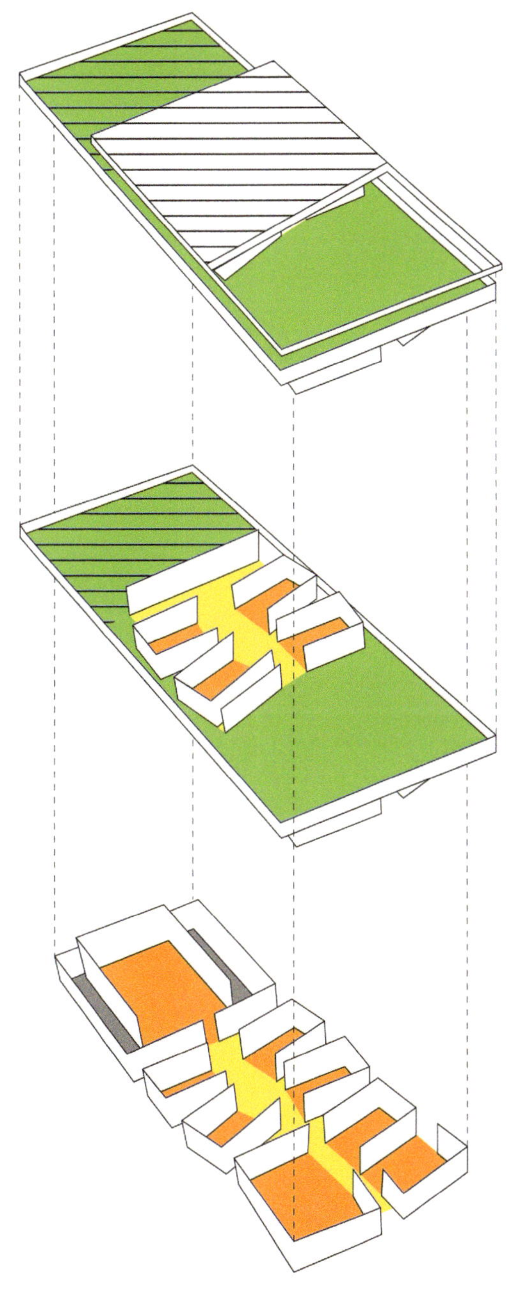

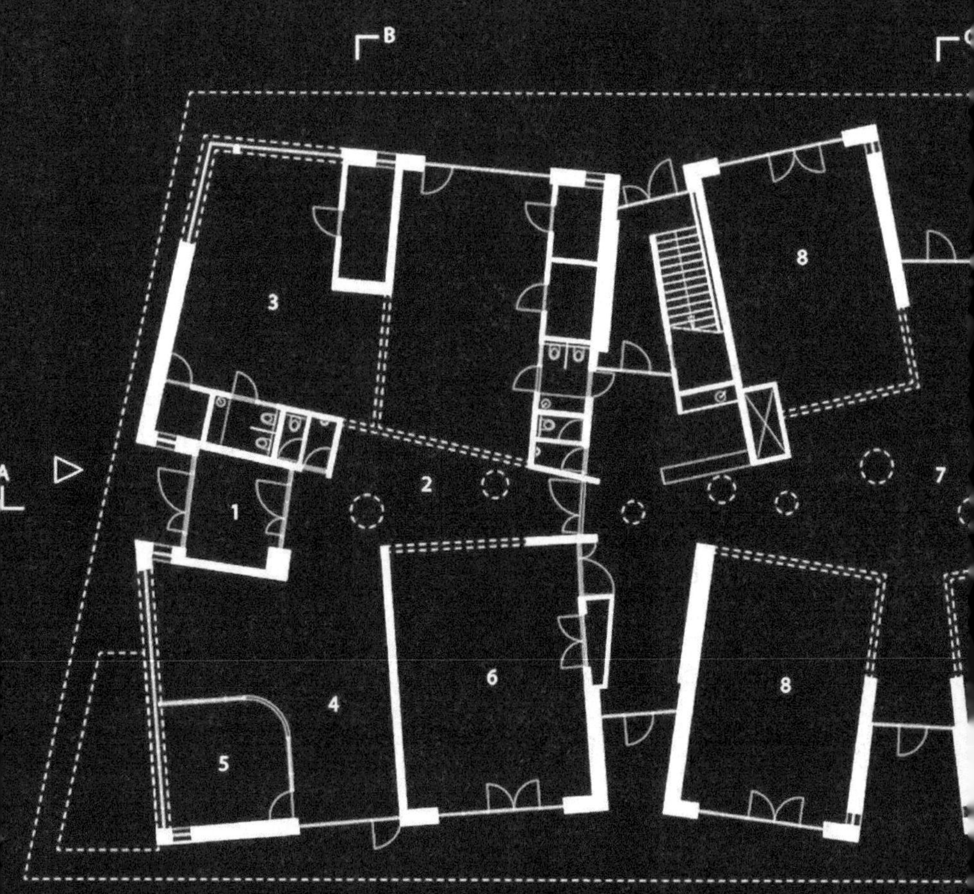

1 Entrance
2 Multifunctional room
3 Day care
4 Reception/library
5 Meeting room
6 Play room
7 Multifunctional room
8 Classrooms
9 Dressing rooms
10 Gym

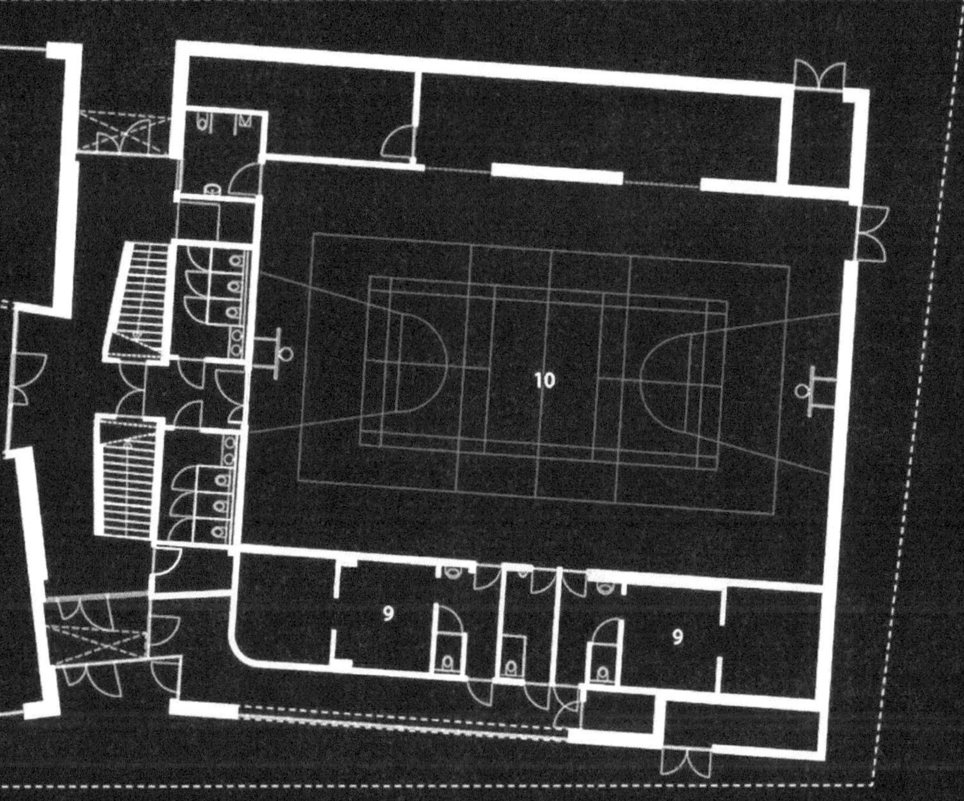

D
D
10
9
9

IKC
De Geluksvogel

School De Brug

In its approach to visualizing education, this school fosters an ambivalence. First of all there is the centric way of education and the concentric arrangement of the school around its pupils. The children form the focal point of the school and the building is literally constructed around them. In its architecture it reflects the way of education whereby children and a sense of community are the main focus of the school.

Children are prepared for a responsible role in society. This connection to the outside world is reflected in the centrifugal arrangement of classrooms around the concentric common space. It's both concentric and centrifugal formal expressions lend the new school an ambiguous identity.

Materials of the now demolished educational buildings that used to occupy the site have been an inspiration for the new concentric school. Corrugated aluminum roofing is echoed in the ribbon that encloses the entire school. The light grey tone of the former school returns in the cement skin brick masonry of the new school.

The school's main entrance and central space are finished in Accoya wood cladding.

A warm and tactile invitation from the heart of the school is the result. Tactile quality of the interior is announced at the main entrance where part of the brick work was carved out and replaced by wood. Sense and color of wood are continued into the central space.

This wooden indoor space supplies an intimate and protective atmosphere. Center of the school is the huge, timber clad skylight that balances on the concrete supporting walls. This skylight also forms a structural hub in the school's roof construction. It is the void that casts daylight along wooden cladding, revealing clouds floating by during the day and letting in starlight at night.

Environmental awareness is a key issue in this MOS school's experience. The volume of the school was made compact in favour of more green space. Recycling and sustainability were introduced in an educational manner by way of water saving measures, a compost heap and other means. By making many processes visible the school building itself becomes an educational tool rather than just a shell.

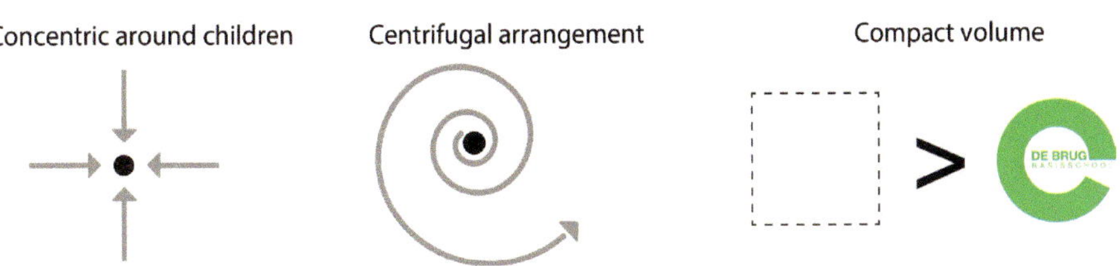

North
0 1 3 6 10 m

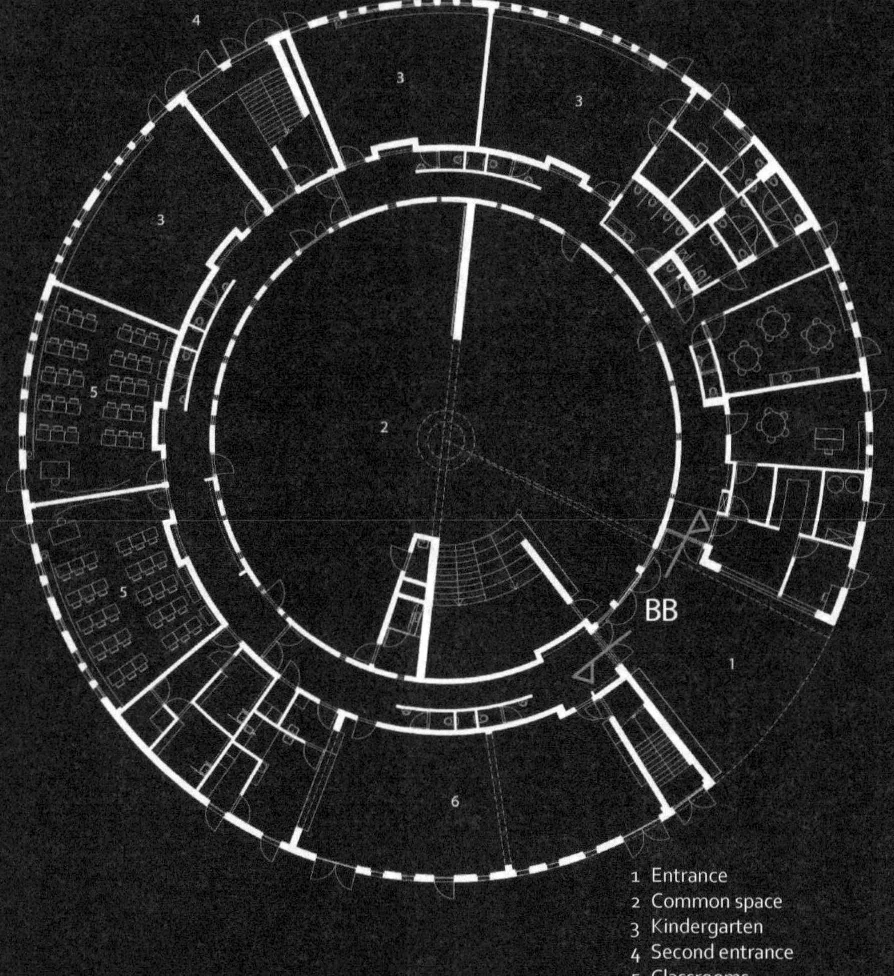

4
3
3
3
5
5
2
BB
1
6
1 Entrance
2 Common space
3 Kindergarten
4 Second entrance
5 Classrooms
6 Restaurant

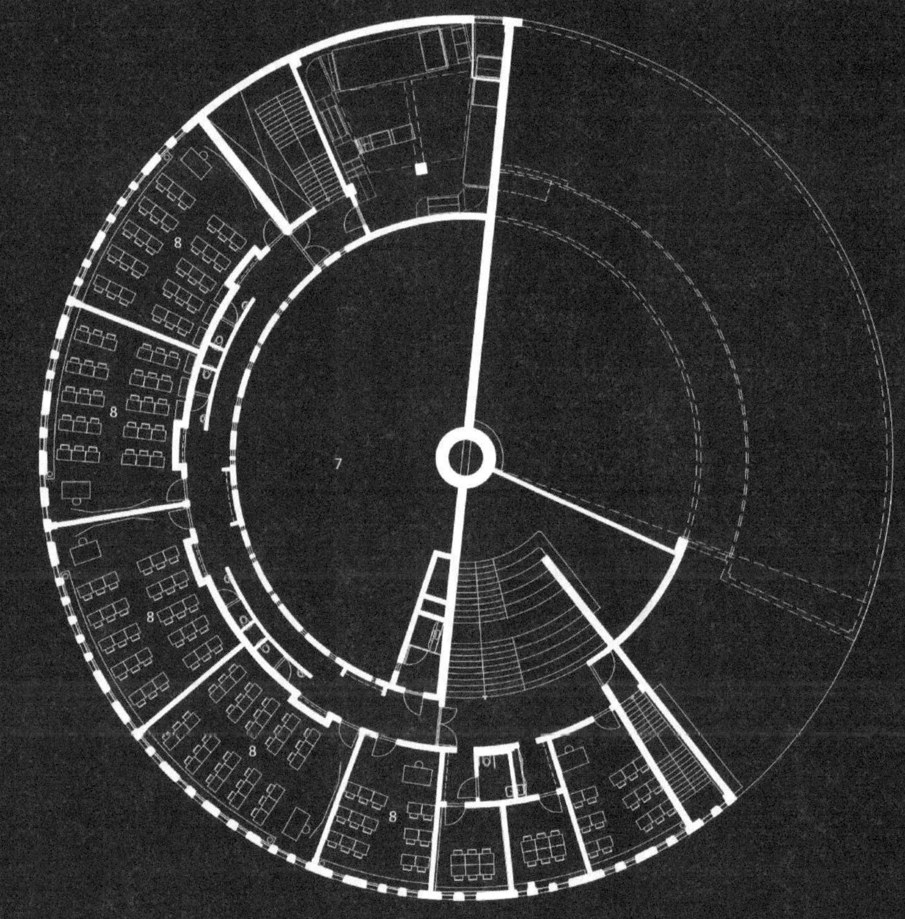

Experience and local culture - The work of UArchitects

Since the COVID-19 pandemic, the Netherlands has been confronted with a number of new, urgent problems. Affordable housing is one of the biggest of these problems and cannot be viewed in isolation from the facilities - like schools and cultural centres - required when affordable housing is constructed. Both can only be addressed in the context of area development.The need to resolve the challenges above is reinforced by a number of developments, one of the most important of which is climate change. It has prompted a major paradigm shift in the field of architecture. UArchitects is at the forefront of this development.UArchitects is very aware that current pragmatic approaches are not helping us achieve the progress necessary. The firm's founder, Misak Terzibasiyan, believes we should challenge architecture to be "more than practical" and that this is the only way to develop a better vision of the built society of the future. Hence the firm's frequent participation in competitions, which give architects the opportunity to discover and explore the possibilities of architecture and also overcome practical and financial constraints. Misak says that competitions give entrants the freedom to sketch new scenarios.

Form and function

Functionalism claimed an autonomy for architectural form by linking it to function and excluding other influences. The slogan was that form followed function. Italian architect Aldo Rossi was the first person to break through this 'naive functionalism', based on the continuity of form in urban situations, amongst other things.There is currently a great urgency to build more with less. For ecological reasons, architects are being challenged to work with existing architecture. The question is how this affects the complex relationship between function and form.

There is a tendency to rashly overestimate and underestimate possibilities in this respect. UArchitects is interested in how people use a particular building but also in the flexible use they will make of buildings in the future. The firm explores the different ways in which buildings can be used for other functions in the future in each and every project.

Utilitarian yardstick
The dichotomy between form and function is front of mind in the exploration process UArchitects undertakes. It is one of a number of firms that have managed to free themselves from this dichotomy. Its architects focus on experience, perception and local culture in the architecture they design.

This is remarkable in a world where every building without exception is measured by a utilitarian yardstick. In other words, buildings are judged solely on the utility they provide. The idea is for buildings to somehow make life more humane and liveable.

However, for many people, life actually feels richer and more liveable if it is not reduced to mere utility. These people appreciate buildings that provide space for various activities, responsibilities and pleasures, even if the utility value of these buildings is not immediately clear.

The quality of spaces like this can be experienced in the impressive series of schools that UArchitects has designed in recent years. One good example is De Geluksvogel in Maastricht, which was designed with the use that children make of time and space in mind. The school's rooms can be used for multiple activities as well.Exciting possibilities are created for architecture if form is not constantly pitted against function. UArchitects' portfolio of work showcase these possibilities in the real subjects of architecture it reveals.

Harm Tilman

ABOUT

Author
Misak Terzibasiyan

The founder and principal Architect of UArchitects (Urban Design and Architects), Misak Terzibasiyan, is personally and professionally focused on an international context as well as the influence of cultural themes. This focus is primarily rooted in his ethnic background, as Misak Terzibasiyan was born in Helsinki, Finland.
He studied at the Eindhoven University of Technology in the Netherlands and gained experience working with several international architectural offices before establishing the company in the cultural and architectural hub of Eindhoven. UArchitects is an international office that embraces diversity, welcoming individuals from various nationalities.

Our investigative approach is evident in the thorough dialogue we engage in with our clients. Our scope for reflection extends beyond the projects themselves; we also delve into the broader cultural context of architecture and urban development. We strive to make a meaningful social contribution by exploring the role and responsibilities of architects in urban design. Sustainability is our primary objective.

Reflection is a valuable tool, especially when interacting with different cultures, as it helps us better comprehend our position regarding universal themes that are integral to society. Understanding the societal identity is crucial for us when we undertake projects in diverse cultures and locations. This approach doesn't adhere strictly to a conventional critical regionalism but is instead an open-minded approach grounded in context and our profession.

Review
Harm Tilman

Harm Tilman (Rotterdam 1954) Urban designer (TU Delft)

Urban Design Coordinator, Rotterdam Academy of Architecture and Urban Design

Editor-in-chief of de Architect (Ten Hagen Stam, Sdu Uitgevers, Vakmedianet)

Lectures at numerous institutions and schools in the Netherlands and abroad.
Publications on modern architecture and spatial planning

VivaArchitectuur.nl, an independent and irregular architecture blog "Architecture is
the experience of it"

PROFILE AND AWARDS

2003
- Foundation of UArchitects on the first of September.

2004
- Publication in Cobouw, concrete workshop
- Publication Wilhelminaplein, Matrix Eindhoven

2005
- Lecture Centre for Architecture, 2x30
- Finals Laboratorium Rotterdam, mediacentre Rotterdam
- Publication De Architect, Living City
- Publication Future Hospitals, Nuclei
- Exposition museum Het Domein Sittard, Sense of places
- Publication BladNAi, Carlow museum

2006
- Lecture Production and Parts, University of Technology Eindhoven
- Debate Cultural identity of Helmond
- Manifestation, The blue carpet

2007
- Publication SMAAK nr 33 Maasberg
- Nomination Award Noord-Brabant Geldrop
- Publication Arquitetura (Brasil) Maasberg
- Publication Transformation Strijp S
- Publication WAN new houses, Dijkmeijer

2008
- Nomination (Award for Architecture City Eindhoven), Grasrijk
- Publication Magazine for wood nr. 3, Oirschot
- Publication Architecture & Detail (China), Maasberg
- Nomination Award Noord-Brabant, Living area, Overloon
- 3thrd Prize 22 Sustainable Houses, Luchen
- Nomination World Architecture Festival 2008 , Maasberg
- 1st Prize Award Noord-Brabant, Category Living & care, Maasberg

2009
- Final round Bauwelt Prize (Germany), Maasberg
- Publication Architecten Web Magazine nr. 2, Maasberg
- Publication Bouwwereld nr. 2, Living area, Overloon Living
- Lecture RWTH Aachen (Germany)
- Lecture CQ 3, University of Technology Eindhoven
- Publication DAX 25, Dijkmeijer

- Publication Remodeled homes (LOFT, Spain), Dijkmeijer
- Publication European Architecture (BRAUN, Zwitserland), Maasberg
- Nomination Architecture Prize Eindhoven, School Hofke
- Nomination Architecture Prize Helmond, Split View
- Nomination World Architecture Festival 2009, Overloon Living

2010
- Publication Nikkei Architecture (Japan), Maasberg
- Publication Architecture Highlight (A&C Limited,China), Maasberg
- 2 Nominations Architecture Prize Venray, housing project Haviklaan
- Nomination Den Bosch, Landscape Vison Engelermeer
- Finals Piraeus Tower Athens (Greece)
- Publication Web DesignIndex nummer 9, website www.UArchitects.com

2011
- Publication Architecture & Design magazine RUM (Zweden), Maasberg
- Publication Building Skin & Details International Book Publishing Center
  China), Maasberg
- Publication Bamboo Magazine (Brazilië), Maasberg
- 1st Prize , Arch School Awards , School 'de Brug' in Bocholt (Belgium)
- Publication Beyond (China), Piraeus Tower
- Publication B1 Magazine (Bangkok), Piraeus Tower
- Publication Future (Spain), Piraeus Tower
- Publication Mark (Netherlands), Piraeus Tower

2012
- Publication Eco Re Modeling Green Architecture (Spain), Wilhelminaschool
- Publication 360 Architecture International (Hong Kong), Split View
- Publication International Design Yearbook Madison (China) , Maasberg
- Publication Phoenix Publishing and Media Group (China), Meander
- Honorable Mention Housing project Wetzsteinareal Singen (Germany)

2013
- Lindenauer Hafen, 2th and 3th Prize in Leipzig (Germany)
  - Iconic Award winner Germany 2013, project Split View (Germany) and Juvenile
    pavilion (Germany)
  - Publication school project De Brug in Bocholt (Belgium)
  - Publication of Split View (China)
  - Invitation of the Dutch Embassy for exhibition and lecture in Tibilisi about Dutch Architecture.

2014
- German Design Award 2014 for Split View (Germany)

- Nomination for the WAF 2014 category education and Wood Prize with School 't Hofke in Singapore
- Award at IDEA TOPS 2014 in the category education with School 't Hofke in Shenzhen (China)
- IDA Design Award : Gold in the Architecture category institutional with School 't Hofke in Los Angeles (USA)

2015
- Book published : CONTEXT_TEXTURE
- WINNER of De Dirk Roosenburg prize 2015, with School 't Hofke.
- Nomination for the WAF 2015 category sports with sportcentre Zaanstad Zuid in Singapore

2016
- American Architecture Prize, Bronze in the category education with the School 't Hofke

2017
- Nomination for the WAF 2017 category school with IKC de Geluksvogel in Berlijn.
- Nomination for Reynaers prijs 2017 with IKC de Geluksvogel.
- WINNER of de Victor de Stuersprijs 2017 (Maastricht) with IKC de Geluksvogel.
- WINNER of American Architecture Prize 2017 in the category education with IKC de Geluksvogel.
- WINNER of MODERN COLLECTIVE LIVING CHALLENGE and the BB Green Award

2018
- Member of the judging panel at the World Architecture Festival 2018 in Amsterdam
- Nomination for Plan IT 2018 with IKC de Geluksvogel

2019
- Second prize for World Architecture & Design Awards 2019 with IKC de Geluksvogel
- Gold Winner of Muse Design Award 2019 with IKC de Geluksvogel
- Honorable mention Architecture MasterPrize with Sport centre Zaanstad Zuid
- Shortlist mention of UK Brick award 2019 with IKC de Geluksvogel
- WINNER in the category Housing up to 5 floors concept with "living among the trees",
- International Residential Architecture Awards 2019
- Second Award in the category housing single family 2019 with "Split View",
- International Residential Architecture Awards 2019
- Rose Gold Winner of Muse Design Award 2019 with School 't Hofke

2020
- Honorable mention Architecture MasterPrize with Living among the trees
- Second Award in the category Educational Built with IKC de Geluksvogel, Global Future Design Award 2020
- Second Award in the category Housing Concept with Living among the tree, Global Future Design Award 2020

- Honorable mention in the category Educational Built with School 't Hofke, Global Future Design Award 2020
- BEST Public Service Architecture Netherlands with IKC de Geluksvogel, European Property Awards Architecture (London)
- WINNER of the Sustainable Skyscaper Design Challenge with Collective Tower Hong Kong
- Runner-up in the category Residential Concept with Collective Tower Hong Kong, Architect of the year Awards 2020
- Runner-up in the category Housing Built with Split View, Architect of the year Awards 2020
- WINNER in the category Institutional Building Built with IKC de Geluksvogel, Architect of the year Awards 2020

2021

- Publication of the book: Experience and Meaning of Architecture
- Shortlisted with a living concept in China Title: Living with Nature
- WINNER of the DIY competition: first prize for the Affordable Home
- Finalist Mention (YAC) Arctic Hotel
- Honourable Mention: The Circle of Life(Bee Breeders)
- WINNER in the category Sport Design Built with Sporthal de Vang, World Design Awards 2021
- WINNER in the category Residential Concept (Multi-Unit) with Collective Tower Hong Kong, World Design Awards 2021
- Second Award in the category Residential Architecture High Rise Concept with Collective Tower Hong Kong, Global Future Design Awards 2021
- WINNER in the with Collective Tower Hong Kong, International Residential Architecture Awards 2021
- WINNER in the with Living in Nature, International Residential Architecture Awards 2021

2022

- Publication of the book: Experience of Architecture and Art
- First Prize European Tender Multifunctional Accommodation Almkerk
- Second Prize invited competition Switzerland
- WINNER Living in Nature , World Design Awards
- WINNER Eco Modular Home, World Design Awards
- WINNER Micro Home, International Residential Architecture Awards
- WINNER The Circle of Life, International Residential Architecture Awards
- WINNER School de Brug, Architect of the Year Awards

2023

- First Prize Buildner (Bee Breeders) with Micro Colony
- Nomination for the WAF 2023 Singapore with the projects Micro Colony, Eco Modular Home and Affordable Biobased Houses
- Micro Colony has WON the WAFX award in the Water category.
- Affordable Biobased Houses has WON the WAFX award in the Building Technology category.
- Micro Colony has WON the GROHE Water Prize 2023.

Source
Pictures on the pages 19 untill 53; Nobert van Onna
The other pictures of Daan Dijkmeijer
Graphics and renders of UArchitects

Website of UArchitects